Brian Powle's Unbelievable World

Brian W. Powle

NHK出版

本書は月刊誌「NHK ニュースで英会話」に連載された英文エッセイ "My Local News around the World" から19編を選んで掲載したものです。

表紙・本文デザイン・DTP	渓上敦司
表紙カバーイラスト	mame&co
本文イラスト	Brian W. Powle
本文（英文・Notes）編集	木嵜正弘
Notes 執筆	山本暎子（編集者・翻訳者）/ 黒田 晶（作家・翻訳者）
校正	Jeff Clark / 山本暎子

Preface

I do hope you find these stories in *My Unbelievable World* interesting and, of course, believable, because all of them did actually happen. According to my information, such 'human interest' stories are more enjoyable to newspaper readers than world events such as trade disputes or violent incidents in distant lands, which they have to read about everyday and find rather monotonous. At least these stories are entertaining.

For example, one incident involved the simple people living in a small, remote village in the north of Scotland. These villagers certainly believed that their modest, middle-aged neighbor had a nice voice as she sang to herself at home and sometimes in the church choir. But they couldn't possibly have believed that, one day, she would become a world-famous prima donna who could eventually demand thousands of dollars for just one concert ... once she had the time to do it! In this book, you will see how she succeeded.

Who would have believed that an athletic, well-built football player for the NFL, Aaron Hernandez, would end up committing suicide in a prison cell? How could it happen? On the other hand, Japanese baseball player Ichiro Suzuki, who was quite shy because of his slender build, managed to retire recently as one of the great heroes of American baseball. The facts behind this comparison are rather interesting, so you can now read the stories of how the

American football tragedy and the 'American Dream' came true. You can read more about these stories in this book as well as many other interesting ones, too.

By the way, if you want to speak English with your foreign friends, these stories provide ideal material and never get out of date. For instance, you could start your conversation like this; "Did you hear about this unbelievable singer from a village in Scotland?" etc., etc.

Well, my own life has also been unbelievable in some ways. For example, at age 18 I was drafted into the British army for the Korean War. But luckily I found myself in the army record section in Kure, Japan. I returned to the UK on a ship called *the Windrush*. It sank just off the coast of Algeria and, after floating around in the sea for four hours, I was rescued by a Dutch freighter. That was an unbelievable experience.

Earlier on in Japan, while I was flying on a small plane from Tokyo to Kure, I commented on the lovely view of Mount Fuji. The American pilot told me, "That means you'll come back again to Japan." I thought he must be wrong, because I didn't see how that could happen after I left the British army.

Well, it DID happen. Twenty-eight years later, I stopped for what I thought would be a short visit to Tokyo on my way to London from San Francisco. That short visit turned out to last 36 years. Unbelievable! During that time, I taught English at three universities, became a journalist for a famous newspaper *the Asahi Evening News*, interviewing prominent people like Yukio Mishima (writer),

Toshiro Mifune (actor), Taiho (yokozuna) and an assortment of other celebrities which included a geisha girl, a gangster and a Zen priest. I even spoke with Queen Elizabeth when she was meeting British residents in Shinjuku Park. When she asked me about my job, I replied, "Teaching the Queen's English, Your Majesty, because that's the BEST English."... And then, I wrote my first book for NHK Publishing 30 years ago with the help of Masahiro Kizaki, who is still my Japanese editor and has participated in the publication of many other books and stories I have written.

I'd like to give you a tip which might make these stories easier to understand: why don't you FIRST read the notes of explanation in Japanese at the back of the book, noting the meanings of difficult words and idioms. Then read the text which should be easier to understand, even when you read it for the first time. Another idea is to analyze the story just by looking at the cartoons. Ask yourself, "Who are the characters in the picture beside the story? What are they doing and why are they doing it? Where are they? " Write down the answers. Then look at the text to check if your answers were right. This too will help you to further memorize useful words and idioms.

Finally, I would really like to thank Mr. Motoi Kusaka, Mr. Masahiro Kizaki and Mr. Masataka Kikuchi for their very great help and encouragement without which this book could not have been completed. Many, many thanks especially to Mr. Kusaka, who greatly helped to make it a success from the initial stages to its completion.

Contents

Two Amazing "Rags to Riches" Stories
  from Scotland 8

Unmade Bed Sells for $4,000,000! 15

Athletes Who Make All the Right Choices
  —and the Wrong Ones 21

The Amazing Story of Willy,
  the Cross-dressing Cuttlefish 27

She Turned Her Dead Husband into
  a Diamond! 32

How Maliwan Transformed
  an "Opium Village" 37

UK's Dangerous Craze For Meerkats as Pets 45

Was the Nanny an Angel or a Devil? 50

One Man's Meat Is Another Man's Poison 58

"Plastic Changed My Life!" 63

From Dog Meat to Crufts Champion 71

Insect Burger, Anyone? 79

Will Elephants Completely Disappear
   in 20 Years' Time? 85

Why Does "Affluenza" Help
   Millionaire Killers? 91

Did a Ray of Sunshine Reveal
   Dark Secrets? 98

Did the Dangerous Alligator Need
   "Anger Management"? 102

It's More Fun in the Philippines ...
   with Lots of Money! 109

Are Cows Causing Climate Change? 117

Improve Your English with Shakespeare! 123

Notes 131

Two Amazing "Rags to Riches*" Stories from Scotland

First I have to make clear that Susan and Joanne, about whom I'm writing, weren't actually wearing rags when they began their remarkable careers, but they *were* living in very poor conditions with almost no hope for the future. So when these ladies ended up as world-famous multimillionaires*, their stories were indeed amazing.

Some time ago, Susan Boyle was born to a mother aged 45, which was then considered very old to have a child. Her early life was not a happy one. She suffered from Asperger syndrome*, which made speech and social contact very difficult for her. Although she had a high IQ, her actions were somewhat clumsy. As a result of this, poor Susan suffered from a lot of bullying at school, which sometimes made her cry. In spite of this, she persevered with* her studies and singing. As she had a naturally beautiful voice, she joined the school choir and did quite well in song contests, but nobody ever thought she was good enough to make a living with her singing.

When her mother died, Susan was so upset* that she stopped singing for a while. However, she eventually started singing to herself at home and thereby preserved her talent. A friend who listened to her singing told her that she was really good. She suggested that Susan should compete in a popular British television contest called "Britain's Got Talent." That program features amateurs who feel they may have enough talent to go professional. It's very competitive, and very few succeed, even if they win. So at first Susan shrugged off the suggestion, saying she certainly wasn't good enough and besides, the return* rail fare from Scotland was too expensive for her. She told her friend that her voice might be good enough for the local choir, but that was all. How wrong she was!

When the great day* of the contest came, Susan arrived at the television station feeling very nervous. She was even more nervous when she had to go on stage and was suddenly confronted by a huge audience and the entertainment celebrities who were there to judge her performance. When overweight, middle-aged Susan nervously ventured on stage*, two of the judges rolled their eyes and smiled cynically. Many in the audience even laughed outright. Why bother to listen?* How could this elderly woman possibly win?

For her song, Susan chose "I Dreamed a Dream," a hit song from a popular London musical. From Susan's first beautiful note, which soared to the ceiling and round the great auditorium, everyone was thunderstruck*. There was no doubt that they were listening to a rare, incredibly beautiful voice. The thunderous* applause that greeted her performance seemed to surprise Susan. Even the judges looked at each other in astonishment. In fact, Susan was already leaving the stage unaware of the impression she had created, when an official ushered her back on because the applause was continuing. Perhaps she thought she really was "dreaming a dream"—but the dream was reality.

Since that time her success has been absolutely non-stop. This middle-aged lady, who used to live in a small Scottish cottage singing to herself, is now in demand in concert halls, recording studios, and television stations around the world. In addition, she's making tens of millions of dollars, though it seems money is not important to her. Actually, I think it's not only her voice that makes her so popular. She projects an air of sincere, innocent simplicity* and has a kind of mature, plump* beauty; she could be anybody's favorite aunt or grandmother. She's really so different from the usual popular singer.

Of course, Susan still has to be careful with her disorder. At Heathrow Airport, for instance, she once had a meltdown* and began shouting, "Help me! Help me! I've done nothing wrong." So airport attendants DID have to help her. But I suppose such an outbreak is not surprising, considering the pressure she's been under in her amazing career, which came so late in her life. The important point is that despite handicaps Susan Boyle has persevered and continued to give joy to millions with her voice.

My next story is about Joanne, who is perhaps even more famous than Susan. Although she comes from a more stable background, she too "had her demons*." As an aspiring writer in Edinburgh, Scotland, she admits that at one time in 1992 she was suffering from clinical depression* and contemplating suicide*. Not surprising, since she was a divorced, penniless single mother on welfare*, and no one seemed interested in her writing.

Now it's difficult to imagine that Joanne ever had these experiences, since she's become an elegant lady who gives millions to charity. Her lodgings* at that time were so poor and cold that she chose to write her novels in restaurants around Edinburgh, including a fish and chip shop; but, like Susan, she just persevered. Her first idea came to her on a train from Manchester to London, which had been delayed by four hours—something quite usual in England though rare in Japan. Quite possibly* it was the most profitable delay in world history, because during that time she got the idea of writing about a bespectacled* little boy named Harry Potter and Hogwarts School of Witchcraft and Wizardry.

As everyone in the world knows, Harry Potter's adventures are wonderful stories, but back then publishers just weren't interested in them. Joanne's literary agent, Christopher Little, showed her 12 rejection slips* from publishers. Finally the comparatively small Bloomsbury Publishing accepted her book, *Harry Potter and the Philosopher's Stone*. She was thrilled to bits*, but in a sense it was just a lucky break. It is alleged that the publisher was on the verge of* rejecting it, when he gave the manuscript to his eight-year-old daughter to read at bedtime. Right from the beginning, she loved the stories and asked for another chapter to read. It seems she was so fascinated that she could hardly put the manuscript down. Her father decided that if his daughter loved it so much, other children would love it too. So he agreed to publish it, offering Joanne Rowling a measly* 1,500-pound advance*. He told her, "Don't expect too much. There's just NO market for children's books like this." Again I have to say, "How wrong he was!"

There's no need to tell you how popular Harry Potter books have become. More than 500 million of them have been sold around the world in over 70 languages. Thousands of readers around the world have waited in line outside bookshops so they could be the first to get a new addition to the series. And of course filmmakers have earned millions, if not billions*, too. Who knows? If that train from Manchester hadn't been delayed for four hours, Harry Potter might never have been born. Perhaps Miss J. K. Rowling was angry at the delay without realizing that behind that inconvenient cloud there was a MASSIVE silver lining*.

Unmade Bed Sells for $4,000,000!

When they first saw Tracey Emin's work of art, many visitors to the Tate Gallery in London thought it was a joke. True to its name*, *My Bed** was a dirty unmade bed*. Surprisingly, however, Emin's work was shortlisted* for the prestigious Turner Prize* in 1999. It didn't win the prize, but it did win its creator a lot of attention*, not all of it positive. As far as I and many others could see, there was nothing beautiful or artistic about the 'sculpture,' if you can call it that.

Not long after it was exhibited at the Tate, the art world received another surprise when famed collector Charles Saatchi paid $250,000 for *My Bed*. They thought he was just crazy.

Well, as it turned out, he was only 'crazy like a fox,' because he's sold *My Bed* later through Christie's*, the auction house, for ... $4,000,000! Of course, he made a huge profit, like many other modern art collectors who, in my opinion, might better be called "investors," since they have more money and business acumen* than good taste. People were surprised once again, because this time the bed sold for more than double the presale estimate. I think it shows that if you know the art business, art is a much better investment than stocks, real estate or commodities.

Of course, in a way, *My Bed* is indeed an incredible artwork, because of the first shocking impression it gives viewers. It's as if a father had walked into his wayward daughter's untidy bedroom* hoping to see her, and instead was confronted with this unpleasant, unmade bed, along with empty bottles of vodka, dirty knickers*, half-filled packets of cigarettes and used condoms strewn about* the carpet next to it. It does convincingly* symbolize the owner's way of life. Yes, I suppose it is an artistic success in that respect*.

In the face of widespread criticism from conservative critics these past 16 years, Tracey Emin is proud and unapologetic*. "I love it," she says. "It even has the same strange smell as it had 16 years ago!" I may be old-fashioned, but I think that smell is the LAST artistic expression I would want*. If, as the saying goes, "Beauty is in the eye of the beholder,"* there must be some strange beholders about nowadays.

There is one thing Emin said that MAY be true. "My work has changed people's perception* of art." I agree. A lot of modern art is just a gimmick*, and *My Bed* puts undeserved value on such ridiculous gimmicks, which masquerade as works of art*. Nowadays, there are many billionaires who have so much money that they really don't know how to spend it all. So they just compete with each other to see who can own the most expensive 'work of art.' At least that's what I understand from reading the opinions of many well-known art critics.

It was first reported that Jay Jopling, an art dealer, was the recent buyer of *My Bed*, but it turns out that he purchased the work on behalf of* a wealthy German. The new owner was, no doubt, faced with an interesting question. If you bought *My Bed*, WHERE on earth would you put it?* I think if you put it in the middle of your living room and held a dinner party, many of your guests would feel uncomfortable and might even lose their appetites! The new owner solved this thorny problem* by loaning the work to the Tate Gallery, where it now resides in unkempt splendor*.

Another artist raking in the millions* is US sculptor Jeff Koons. One of his very successful gimmicks is to make a series of huge colored stainless steel sculptures called "Balloon Dogs." At an auction on November 12, 2013, just one of these sculptures fetched* $58.4 million, a price which seems to make *My Bed* a bargain*. As you can see from my cartoon, there's nothing cute about Koons' dogs. When first seen, they just look like a series of balloons which could be arranged by any child at a party. What the buyers get is a huge 'arranged' lump of stainless steel, which I think could be better used to make saucepans, knives or at least something useful. Well, who knows? The purchaser may turn out to be very clever and sell it for $100 million in ten years time.

Martin Arts is another modern artist who has caused an 'explosion' in the art world. He recently sold a crazy-looking painting, whose

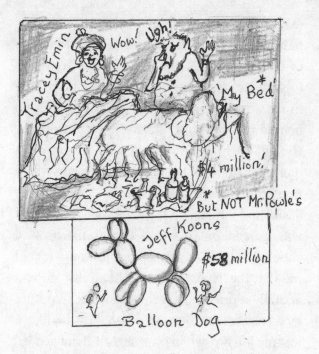

title I can't say here because it's too vulgar*. Anyway, you couldn't possibly guess what it's supposed to be. He caused an 'explosion' because he sold it for $21,000,000 on eBay*, the first time such a high-priced painting had been sold through that source.

Modern art can cause a lot of confusion, as I can tell you from a personal experience I had in a modern art gallery in Mexico City. I was exhausted after looking at a lot of contemporary paintings, which I thoroughly enjoyed in spite of their modern style. I saw a very inviting-looking* chair, where I sat to rest my weary limbs. Suddenly, someone came running up behind me shouting, "Please! Please! Don't sit there!" I thought perhaps I had sat on a dangerous tarantula spider* or perhaps a still more poisonous black widow*. I was very afraid and jumped up from the chair. But there was no reason to fear. The man who had shouted at me was a museum curator. He told me that the 'chair' on which I had just sat was actually a priceless piece of modern sculpture by a celebrated* Mexican artist. "I would have lost my job if you had even slightly damaged it," he complained. I apologized and added, "Well at least it was useful. It helped me to relax."

Athletes* Who Make All the Right Choices – and the Wrong Ones

At the age of 23, it looked as if Aaron Hernandez had everything going for him. Everyone told him, "The world is your oyster.*" At least that's how it looked on the surface, as by that time he was already an American football star.

At that young age, Hernandez was certainly one of the most talented players in the NFL*. No one was surprised that he was in line to sign* a contract worth $40 million with the Patriots, one of the most famous teams in the country. His personal life then was also a very happy one. When he went home to his luxurious million-dollar mansion*, he was greeted by his beautiful fiancée* and three-year-old daughter, who both loved him dearly*. In fact, wherever he went he was loved and warmly greeted by thousands of fans and friends. What more could a young man want?

Yet* only three years later, early in 2017, a

tragedy occurred. The dead body of Hernandez, covered with tattoos, was discovered on the floor of a dark prison cell*. He had committed suicide by hanging himself with a sheet.* What had gone so badly wrong* for him in the previous few years? Why had this terrible incident happened to a young athlete of such promise*?

It seems that from the time he was 18, Hernandez was making all the wrong choices. Instead of socializing with boys and girls of his own age at dances and parties, he preferred to mix with young gang members* who were into taking drugs, carrying guns, and drinking too much alcohol while barhopping* around town. That was the beginning of his descent into hell*. Finally, the low point of his life* came when he murdered a good friend, Odin Lloyd, by shooting him at night in a deserted* field near his mansion after giving him a ride* in a car. That was his worst choice. In fact, some months before, he had almost killed* another friend by shooting him in the face. Luckily this friend survived, although he was permanently blinded in his right eye*. Because of

Hernandez's fame and money, this case was hushed up*, and he was not immediately prosecuted for it. If he had been, a life might have been saved.*

Anyway, after he was arrested for the first-degree murder* of Odin Lloyd, Hernandez was found guilty* and sentenced to life in prison without the possibility of parole*. It's difficult to pin down* any real motive for Lloyd's murder, but probably Hernandez was high on drugs* at the time and imagined he had been insulted* in some way. He was a very touchy type of person* who imagined insults when none were intended. But why did he commit suicide in prison? As they say, "While there's life, there's hope*," no matter what the circumstances. Well, I suppose that after enjoying such a luxurious lifestyle, Hernandez might have become depressed at the thought of having to spend the rest of his life in a tiny, dark prison cell with criminals as his only friends, and not so surprisingly suicide seemed like a solution.

Actually, Hernandez is not the only member of the Patriot's football team to get on the

wrong side of the law*. Many other members have been prosecuted for violent abuse of some kind or another, which unfortunately seems to be a common characteristic of arrogant, overpaid sportsmen* around the world. For instance, after making a bad scene* in a nice hotel, a drunken British footballer* was told by a bartender to behave himself*. The footballer replied, "Don't speak to me that way. I earn more money in one day than you do in a year, so f--- off*!" I'm happy to say that the footballer was later arrested for his rowdy* behavior.

Anyway, there is one professional athlete who has certainly made all the right choices, including his decision to move from Japan to the USA. I am speaking of none other than the renowned baseball player Ichiro Suzuki. Although he has a very common Japanese name, he is really a most uncommon* man.

With his small build* and often unconventional* swinging style, Ichiro was advised early on* by one of his coaches that he could never be a really great player. But he ignored this negative advice and made the right decision to continue playing baseball until he became a professional. Unlike Hernandez, who was often absent from training sessions, Ichiro made a decision to never be absent. Instead of partying* and taking drugs, Ichiro decided to exercise his body until it was so limber* he could meet any challenge that occurred during the course of the game*. He has told his young admirers*, "You don't have to be a muscular hunk* to get on in baseball*. You can be a regular guy with a regular build like me. Never give up."

Moreover, he just liked to be called by his given name of "Ichiro," as seen on his uniform, rather than his surname of "Suzuki," another choice which was pleasantly unconventional. Ichiro retired in March 2019. Due to his right choices and everyday exercise routine, he did not suffer a major injury, with the result that he achieved an outstanding record. As Albert Camus*, the French novelist, said, "Your life is the sum of all your choices.*"

I'm afraid this saying also applies to Hernandez, someone who made all the wrong choices. To look at his movie-star good looks and huge muscular body, most people would certainly have predicted a great future for him as an athlete. But, as they say, "Handsome is as handsome does.*" In this sense, Ichiro is handsome, but Hernandez was not.

The Amazing Story of Willy, the Cross-dressing Cuttlefish

Scientists in universities in South Australia are studying the amazing mating behavior* of the highly intelligent cuttlefish*. They have discovered that cuttlefish are a cross-dressing, or transvestite* species, one that has the ability to change shape, color and skin texture*. Males can look like females if they want to. They use this unique talent to get just what they want — even girlfriends! Many scientists surmise* that cuttlefish may even have brains to analyze and work out* problems in a logical way.

If a human male or female wishes to look and behave like the opposite sex, it's a very complicated and expensive process, but this is NOT the case with the lucky cuttlefish. In the blink of an eye*, they can change their shape and color into anything they want, and often that means becoming a member of the opposite sex.

Having read up on* research done by Australian universities and the Victoria

Museum in London, I have written a short story about Willy, a cuttlefish who finds a beautiful girlfriend through cunning and daring*. I'm not sure whether it's a completely true story, but perhaps it could be.

Willy was a small cuttlefish who lived off the south coast of Australia. The trouble was, Willy was so small that he couldn't get his tentacles* anywhere near the beautiful lady cuttlefish who were swimming around him in erotic circles. Willy didn't dare get too close*, because the ladies were protected by male cuttlefish. These guards were much bigger than Willy, and their bullying poses* suggested that they could easily beat him up or even kill him.

Willy was desperate, because a cuttlefish's lifespan is so short, a mere 18 months or so. If he didn't do something soon, he might die a virgin*. What a thought! Faint heart never won fair lady. How could he get through* that gang of giant cuttlefish that were swimming between him and the beauty he wanted so badly to know*?

So he discussed his problem with his best friend Freddy, who always seemed to have so much success with the 'girls.' Freddy advised Willy to use his brains. "First," Freddy said, "you must be willing to cross gender lines*. You can change your appearance into anything you want, so turn off those bright male body lights and stripes. After that, change the color of your skin to a dull brown*, the female color, so the large bullies will think you ARE a female. They won't attack you, because they won't see you as competition*. Then you'll be free to approach the beauty of your choice*."

So that was what Willy did. He turned off his striped male lights and, for all intents and purposes*, looked like a female. At first, he was very afraid of all the big cuttlefish bullies swimming all around. It was especially scary when one of them swam very near to him, mistaking him for a female, and sought a bit of romance*, which of course Willy rejected. After some close calls*, he was safely in the presence of* a particularly beautiful cuttlefish. This was the one for him, but she didn't seem interested. Naturally, she thought that Willy, with his new shape and colors, was a female. Once he figured that out*, Willy turned on his bright

Willy strikes while the iron is HOT

lights and changed back to his male shape. For both of them, it was "love at first sight*." She turned away from a giant cuttlefish who had been courting* her, and lovingly put her tentacles around Willy, who was now in the Seventh Heaven* of happiness. Willy's gender-bending adventure turned out to be well worth the risk*!

Actually, studies show that female cuttlefish accept 70% of the transvestite cuttlefish who want to mate with them, and only 30% of the non-transvestite cuttlefish. This is important, because there are ten times more males than females*. Why this is, no one knows: perhaps the females think the daring cross-dressers are braver and have more sex appeal. So, not only will Willy have moments of sexual ecstasy, he can be sure that in the future there will be many baby Willys swimming around. However, because of the Australians' growing love of Japanese cuisine, many of his children may end up in sushi shops.

Willy is clever in other ways, and he's fast, too. When an enemy is chasing him, he confuses it by letting off a cloud of thick black ink in its face*, so in seconds he can escape. If Willy is hungry and sees a small shrimp or crab on the seabed, he ejects a powerful stream of water at it, so the small creature can't burrow* under the sand for protection. And again it only takes seconds for Willy to grab his lunch. So, whether it's enjoying romance, facing an enemy, or hunting for food, Willy "strikes while the iron is hot*."

She Turned Her Dead Husband into a Diamond!

When Glynis Barnett's husband died of liver and throat cancer* at age 64, she was just devastated*. They'd been happily married for 42 years, so her feelings were quite natural. After his cremation*, the funeral company delivered his ashes* to her home in a small, rather ugly urn*. Her husband had said he didn't care where his ashes were to be scattered*. It was up to Glynis. He said that he just didn't want to be buried in a depressing cemetery.

Since the word "cemetery" has come up*, it is interesting to note that there are a few differences between British and American vocabulary concerning death. Frankly, I think the American versions sound more sensitive at this sad time. Here are a few different examples for you to remember: cemetery (Br.*), memorial garden (Am.*); to die (Br.), to pass on (Am.); coffin* (Br.), casket* (Am.); the body

(Br.), the loved one (Am.). Somehow I think it sounds pleasanter when you ask somebody, "When did your friend pass on?" (Am.) than "When did he die?" (Br.). Something about "die" sounds too final. Actually, British and American vocabularies are interchangeable*, so these are not really strict rules. I think British and Americans both say, "May I offer my condolences* (or sympathy)," to a friend or relative of the deceased*.

Anyway, let's get back to Glynis' problem about what she should do with her husband's ashes. As her husband, John, had been fond of gardening, she thought she would bury his ashes under an old oak tree where he often liked to sit. "To be or not to be?" That was the question, as Hamlet had said when wondering whether to commit suicide or not. In the end it was "not to be," because she thought that if she had to move into a different house, she would have to leave John behind.

Then she found out about ways to dispose of* ashes from the Phoenix Memorial Company in Manchester. An executive of that company told her that they could convert her husband's ashes into* a diamond* ring. She was a bit surprised at first, but was told that it is quite a common method nowadays. Also, it is quite easy, as human ashes and diamonds have a similar carbon content*, although the chemical process used for the conversion is quite complex. They said it would take three months and cost about $10,000 per carat*, 40% cheaper than a natural diamond. The quality would be almost the same. Glynis agreed.

Actually, Glynis was thrilled* when her canary yellow* diamond was delivered—that is the usual color when ashes are used. Her friends were a bit surprised, to put it mildly, when she proudly showed them her diamond ring, explaining, "My dead husband is in there. This way he can ALWAYS be with me." She liked to see their reaction. Her children were a bit dubious* about the idea at first, but later, with a bit of persuasion, they came round* and agreed with her decision. She told her daughter, "I'll leave money to you when I die (pass on), so you can have my ashes converted to diamonds. I use the plural*, because you may want to have my ashes set in* matching

This way he's ALWAYS with me.

canary yellow diamond earrings. That way, you can always have your father AND your mother with you." Of course, this may seem a funny conversation. I don't know whether her daughter agreed, but many of us may be confronted* by the same problem concerning the ashes of 'a loved one' later on.

Some people may think it is not appropriate to discuss or write anything to do with* death or funerals, but actually it's just another human problem which has to be confronted sooner or later, and should not just 'be swept under the carpet*.' In parts of Asia, even humor and laughter at funerals are quite expected. I think this is a very healthy attitude*.

Of course, funeral companies have thought up many other creative, if rather expensive, ways of disposing of the "loved one's" remains*. Ashes can be encased* in a glass paperweight* as a desk decoration, embedded* into an artificial coral reef at sea with fish swimming around it, or sent up into the sky in a self-exploding hot air balloon*. One interesting idea is to have ashes enclosed in a rocket that is part of a beautiful firework display. Everybody can enjoy that. I can imagine one onlooker* saying, as the rocket takes off with Harry's ashes, "Old Harry wanted to go higher and quicker than anybody else. Now his wishes have come true." Anyway, it's a fact that a lot of modern-minded people prefer 'happy' funerals to miserable ones, as it may reflect their joyful lifestyle.

How Maliwan Transformed an "Opium Village"

About 40 years ago, Maliwan Nakrobphai was a 7-year-old girl living in the dirt-poor* village of Ban Huai Hom, high in the mountains of northern Thailand. Although her family grew rice, they were so poor that often they didn't even have enough rice for themselves. Little Maliwan knew what hunger was.

In that area, most of the land where rice should have been growing was instead* used for cultivation of opium poppies*, because opium was much more profitable. The villagers didn't get much money from opium, however, because its production was controlled by gangs who took most of the profits. The village was in a sorry state*, as many of the men who should have been harvesting rice became opium addicts and just lay about in poor dark huts while the women and children starved. Apparently, that is a common situation in the countryside of Afghanistan today. It seemed that nothing could change that sad situation. Anyway, who cared about changing a small village in the mountainous area of Thailand with its many minority peoples?

As Maliwan grew up, she helped to improve this sorry state of affairs, even though she had received little formal education. Now, amazingly, she and her village have business connections with specialized outlets* all over the world, including the United States and Europe. In addition, she lectures regularly in Bangkok about her business methods. Her once impoverished* village has been transformed into* a model community visited by the Thai royal family and foreign tourists. How did she effect this incredible transformation?

Actually, when Maliwan was growing up, the village wasn't completely dominated by opium production. American missionaries lived there for a while and provided the villagers with a very basic education. Before they left, the missionaries gave the village a ram* and six ewes*, as well as some arabica coffee* plants. The villagers looked after* them carefully, but it was Maliwan who put these "missionary gifts" to full use* with great assistance from the Thai royal family.

It seems that the Queen herself was upset that so much land had been deforested* to grow opium, a crop that brought no benefits to the poor people. The royal family in Thailand is so respected that anything they suggest is treated almost like a divine command*. Because of the royal influence, many villagers gave up growing* opium and began engaging in* useful agriculture. This included cultivating the arabica coffee seedlings*, which thrived* in the 20°C temperature of the fresh mountain air. Then with the encouragement and leadership of Maliwan, they also reared* more sheep. They even tackled* the difficult task of getting wool from these sheep, turning it into yarn*, and dyeing* the yarn with natural dyes produced from ground coffee*, mango leaves, turmeric*, and indigo*. Sheep placenta* body lotion and coffee soap are also popular byproducts*.

Because the production of coffee was so successful, Maliwan formed the "Coffee

Processing Group of Ban Huai Hom" to maintain the high quality of the coffee beans farmed by the 60 families who were members. This was further assisted by the royal family, and became part of the Mae La Noi Royal Project, founded to assist the hill peoples. Eventually the taste of this organically grown, high-quality arabica coffee was so appreciated* internationally that it was exported to Europe and the States. For instance, Starbucks* has been a buyer of the green beans since 2002.

The export of naturally dyed woolen* products, such as large shawls*, caps, scarves and bed sheet covers, has been extremely successful, too. At first these woolen products were not greatly appreciated, because people found them to be a bit itchy to the skin*. After hearing about this, the Queen gave the village 70 Australian sheep of the Bond breed. As a result, the quality of the wool has greatly improved, becoming soft and silky to the touch. Maliwan thinks that as long as a useful product is of the highest quality*, it is bound to sell* well. She says, "Don't complain about what you HAVEN'T got; make the most of what you

HAVE got. Many people thought we couldn't do much with just a few sheep and coffee seedlings. Now we have an international business." Many Asian country folk* think they have to go to the cities to be successful. Maliwan has proved that this isn't the case.

In fact, she is determined to improve the quality of the coffee still more by cultivating "civet* coffee." The production of this rare coffee, which sells for up to $500 a kilo on the international market, has a rather interesting story behind it. If you don't know about it, you'll never guess how it's made. The civet is a cute little creature about the size of a small rabbit, and is mostly found in the jungles of Sumatra. Civets are said to choose the best wild coffee beans as food. Once the beans are in the civet's body, they come in contact with amino acids* and various digestive fluids*. This is what gives the beans their special flavor. The beans excreted whole* in the civet's feces* are picked out to make the world's most expensive coffee! Who would believe it?

I'm not sure whether the wealthy drinkers of this coffee know how it is produced—or

whether they would want to know! You might wonder how it was first discovered that civets were able to produce such coffee beans. It seems that some time ago, Dutch colonialists in Sumatra imported expensive coffee bushes* from abroad, and they forbade* the local Sumatran natives to have access to the beans from those bushes. But the natives, who were cleverer than their colonialist masters, noticed that civets excreted coffee beans which seemed completely intact*. They picked them out, cleaned them, and roasted them to make the delicious civet coffee now appreciated worldwide!

Anyway, Maliwan is raising civets for this purpose and presently has eight of them. At her homestay, she offers a cup of arabica coffee for 25 baht (70 cents), while a cup of civet coffee goes for* 100 baht ($2.80). A kilo of civet coffee costs 5,000 baht ($138), while arabica is a mere 350 baht ($10). These prices are still very cheap compared with those in the States and Japan. So it seems that civet coffee must be very profitable in the future.

BUT ... would you really want to pay so much for a cup of coffee? Coffee experts say there is nothing special in the flavor except that it might be a smoother drink*. People may go for it* just because it's a rare and famous product, not for the actual taste. It's similar to wine. For instance, sometimes at a wine tasting session, experts rate quite common, inexpensive wines higher than expensive vintage* grades. Why? Because the tasters have not been allowed to see the labels. Moreover, in places like Sumatra, many civets kept for the purpose of excreting beans live under very cruel conditions; they live in small cages and are almost half starved. So it is natural that coffee from these poor animals doesn't always taste very nice.

However, Maliwan loves and looks after her civets very carefully, so I wouldn't hesitate to buy a cup of HER civet coffee, even though I know HOW, WHY and WHERE it's been produced. How about YOU?

UK's Dangerous Craze* For Meerkats* as Pets

After a UK TV commercial for an insurance company featured a cartoon version of a lovely meerkat called Aleksandr Orlov*, there has been a sudden demand* for these cute little animals as pets. Pet shops seem to have sold thousands of them.

Yes, they LOOK so cute, but this sudden craze can be dangerous for potential owners*. If just one meerkat is purchased, he'll soon feel very lonely and frustrated. In time* he may get angry and give someone a nasty bite*, passing along* the poisonous bacteria* that these animals have in their mouths.

Meerkats are used to being in large groups of 20 to 50, which roam* the Kalahari Desert of Southern Africa, their natural habitat*. A lot of purchasers may think they're like cats, as their names imply*, but they are not similar at all. Cats have been the pets of humans for thousands of years, dating from the time of the ancient Egyptians. Nowadays, meerkats have more or less come straight from the desert to fulfill their role as pets for modern society.

Kimmy Rudland, a student of zoology*, says that meerkats really should not be sold as pets to people who do not understand their ways. She understands them very well and has a pair: Lola, a female, and Lawrence, a younger male. She says Lola is a gentle creature; she likes nothing better than to cuddle up to Kimmy under her duvet*. Like a cat, she really enjoys being stroked*. On the other hand, Lawrence seems to be hyperactive*, running around all over the place, trying to dig a hole in the carpet as if it was the desert soil, or rubbing up against* the furniture and leaving a nasty stain—and an even nastier smell! If any food is left around, he will find it and eat it. He is really quite naughty*.

Can you guess what Lola and Lawrence both enjoy? They can stay still for quite a long time watching television, especially programs featuring animals, like Birmingham's famous Crufts Dog Show*. Of course, their favorite is that of the cartoon character Aleksandr Orlov

Lola and Lawrence watching Aleksandr Orlov on TV

with whom they seem to identify*. Whether they see the same images of him as we do, though, is difficult to say.

Another problem for meerkat owners is that their upkeep* is quite expensive. Kimmy says they need a special diet* of fresh fruit, meat, vegetables and insects, which costs approximately $250 a month. You have to catch the insects yourself, which is rather time-consuming, unless you live in Thailand, where people also eat insects. And meerkats themselves are not cheap; they cost around $1,000 each, depending on the point of purchase*. Anne Davis, an expert on meerkat behavior, is actually glad they ARE expensive, because it stops parents from buying these cute creatures on impulse* after their children have seen the cartoon of Aleksandr Orlov on TV. It seems many children say, "I want a meerkat like Aleksandr for my birthday." A good parent must know when to say "No," whether it's for candy or meerkats.

Dawn Wade, another owner, says she's never had any trouble with her meerkats, though she always wants to be present* when her children are playing with them. The fact that she has four meerkats means they stay happy, as they are never lonely. If a stranger comes to the house, one of them acts as a "sentry*," standing up to see what the danger might be. The others run off to hide* until they hear the "sentry" make a barking noise, which means everything is OK and they can come out of hiding. This routine comes from the desert, where the sentry is on the lookout for* snakes, eagles, jackals and other enemy predators* who might devour a meerkat for a tasty dinner. Also, meerkats get highly nervous of anything flying above them, even airplanes, which they may mistake for an eagle, a particularly dangerous bird for them. So, if you live near an airport, you CAN'T own a meerkat. Anyway, there is no doubt they are highly intelligent animals, but it is better just to watch them on TV rather than to buy them as pets.

Was the Nanny* an Angel or a Devil?

You would think that when a middle-class family fired* their children's nanny for various reasons, it wouldn't even be local news, let alone* national news. However, now the story has been released to media around the world, and it is an unusual one.

When the Bracamonte family needed a nanny for their three children in their nice Upland, California, home, they advertised on Craigslist*, a social media outlet*. Craigslist is quite cheap to use, but for that very reason, users have had many problems. The Bracamonte family found this out the hard way*. When Diana Stretton, 64, applied for the job of nanny, she seemed ideal to Mrs. Bracamonte. She had good references* and looked like everybody's idea of a kindly, beautiful grandmother. But as they say, 'You can't judge a book by its cover.*'

At first Ms. Stretton fit into* the daily

routine as if she were actually a family member. She helped out with everything, and was so good with the Bracamonte's three children that their little boy said, "I want to marry you when I grow up." She seemed like a real treasure.

Unfortunately, after three weeks the relationship with the nanny started to sour*. She did less and less work, until finally she did nothing at all except to come out for her meals. She claimed she was sick, but wouldn't see a doctor. Having adopted a sullen* attitude, Ms. Stretton seemed like an entirely different person. Gradually, life with her became unbearable for the Bracamonte family. Even the little boy said he didn't want to marry her now. Eventually, she didn't even come out of her room except to raid* the icebox for food.

Finally, Mrs. Bracamonte wrote Ms. Stretton a letter stating that as she wasn't fulfilling her duties, she had to leave the house ASAP*. Ms. Stretton replied that she wasn't going anywhere as she now had 'established residency'* in their home and legally she had every right to stay. Furthermore, she wanted the whole family out of the house from 8 am to

8 pm, so she could feel comfortable! She told them to turn down the volume on their TV, as it annoyed her.

Mrs. Bracamonte was furious. "The nanny can't do this to us," she said. "It's OUR house, for heaven's sakes*! I will take legal action to get her out."

She went to the police to get her evicted*, only to find out that there were legal complications*. The family didn't pay Ms. Stretton any money, but had agreed to give her bed and board* in exchange for her doing 20 hours of light work per week. Even though the nanny wasn't fulfilling these services, in the eyes of* the law, she had 'established residency.' The only way to get her out was to initiate a lawsuit*, which would be very expensive and could take many months.

Then the Bracamontes had an idea. They put a padlock on* the icebox door, so the nanny couldn't just help herself to their gourmet food* whenever she felt like it. That seemed to do the trick*, as she suddenly disappeared from the house. However, she left all her personal things in her room and took the key to the house* with

her. It meant that she could just let herself into the house at any time she liked. This idea made the family more nervous than ever. Now they are thinking of changing the lock, if they are allowed to do so by law.

So that's how the situation stands* as I'm writing this. In the meantime*, Diana Stretton was interviewed by a public network and allowed to give HER side of the story. She said that Mrs. Bracamonte made her work very hard for very long hours, much more than 20 hours a week. The family abused* her physically and verbally*, even though they knew she was a frail*, elderly lady. She said they didn't care that the hard work was affecting her weak heart and her aching legs. All she got in exchange was a tiny room and a bit of food. "All they wanted was SOMETHING for NOTHING*," she claimed, adding that they knew she was homeless and had been living out of a car* for the past eight years. They thought they could exploit* her. She wasn't going to let that happen.

Well, those are the two sides to the story. I think I believe the Bracamonte's version. In the past few years, Ms. Stretton has been involved in so many law cases, she has been officially titled* 'a vexatious litigant*.' In other words, she has been a great nuisance to many families in the past by using the law in a frivolous* way.

My family also had a similar, if not worse, problem with our 'tenant from hell.' We rented our family home to an actor and his wife. When he divorced her, she claimed she couldn't pay the rent—but she didn't move out. So she lived there rent-free for four years, until we practically had to 'give' her the house by agreeing to sell it to her for about 10% of the real value, because my mother was getting so worried about the situation. One time, I went to the house asking the woman who was 'squatting*' there to pay at least part of the rent to help with my mother's expenses. She seemed nice enough, apologized, and said she would pay some rent. The next day I got a call from our stupid house agent. He said, "You've been cruelly harassing* the tenant of your house, and threatening her with violence if she didn't leave the house. She'll take legal action if you do it again." I asked him if he really believed her blatant* lies. Well, he did until I explained the situation.

This only goes to show that you have to be very, very careful with the people you meet through Internet sources like Craigslist. For example, one girl in UK fell in love with a young man she thought was an accounting* student at Oxford University. He sent her his photo by e-mail and wrote her many romantic letters.

He seemed to be a handsome young man with a good future before him, so when he asked for money—quite a lot of it—to complete his studies, she gladly sent it to him, even without meeting him personally. In the end, of course, she saw neither him nor her money again. They say that if something is too good to be true, it usually is.*

Luckily, in Japan even wealthy families tend not to have nannies, because many Japanese mothers want to look after their families themselves. Westerners think more Japanese women should have responsible office jobs, as if that would somehow make their lives better. Not everybody agrees. As one housewife in Tokyo told me, "Why would I want to stand in a train three hours a day commuting to work? Why would I want to spend long hours staring at a computer and compete with my male colleagues for an executive position? I just love cooking, looking after my children, and occasionally meeting my friends to play tennis. Me in an office? NO thank you."

Actually, I too had a nanny when I was very

young. I loved her dearly and called her "Fraulein," because she was German. It was my mother's idea to get a nanny. It seems two of my mother's friends had beautiful German nannies, so my father was not against the idea. He said, "I'll go down to London to meet her myself at Victoria Station." He waited on the station platform, where he saw many beautiful ladies, but none of them approached him. Finally, a very plain* lady with pebble-thick glasses* DID approach him saying, "You are wearing the red muffler by which I can identify you. YOU must be Mr. Powle." Well, I suppose my father was a bit disappointed to meet such a plain lady. But it was MY MOTHER who had chosen the nanny from a selection of photos, and she had been careful not to pick a beauty. Anyway, Fraulein was always beautiful in MY eyes.

One Man's Meat Is Another Man's Poison*

One of the problems between Jews* and Muslims* living in Israel has been the calls to prayer, emanating from the mosques* situated throughout the country. Using many decibels* of power through loudspeakers situated at the top of minarets*, these azans* (calls to prayer) start from 5 am. They wake up not only 'the faithful*' but also many non-Muslims, who may not exactly appreciate this unavoidable religious 'alarm clock.'

In response to this, Israeli* Prime Minister Benjamin Netanyahu is backing a bill banning the use of loudspeakers* for this purpose from 11 pm to 6 am, which seems reasonable. In fact, not a few non-Muslims think the ban should be extended to 9 am*. However, many Muslims are very angry about it. Mr. Mafeed Shawana says, "It upsets me. The calls to prayer have been going on* for 1,400 years. It's our religious right." Since

Israel was developed on land that mostly belonged to Muslim Arabs, he has a point.*

Actually, I myself am a bit sympathetic to* the Israelis. That's because while I was on holiday on the beautiful island of Bali, where the Hindu religion still dominates*, I was invited to a riotous* party, which lasted until three in the morning. After that, I had hoped to have many hours of sweet dreams. Alas for* my hopes! Like the people in Israel, I was suddenly woken up at 5 am by a booming* call to prayer, echoing* from a minaret that had recently been built right next to the hotel. It seemed to go on forever, so I couldn't get a wink of sleep* after that.

The manager of the hotel told me, "Yes, we've asked the imam* of the mosque to tone it down, but he says 'the faithful' need the azans and they're more important than tourists. Unfortunately, with the huge donations that the mosque receives from Saudi Arabia*, they have just invested in* new high-tech speakers, which they turn up to full volume. Because of this, I have fewer guests and I'm losing money, but there's absolutely nothing I can do. We

Hindus in Bali are a minority here in Indonesia, where Muslim laws prevail*."

However, it may surprise you that there was one time when I actually ENJOYED listening to the calls to prayer! That was when I was taking a Nile River cruise during the sunset hours. The azans from the beautiful minarets on the banks* of the Nile seemed to dramatize the exotic desert landscape*, which has hardly changed in thousands of years. On that occasion, the melodious* azans helped to make it an unforgettable experience for us tourists, as we slowly cruised down the river.

Another place where I had a similar "religious" noise problem was in Puerta Vallarta, Mexico. I was inspecting a room in the old part of the town, with the idea of staying there for a month or more to complete a book. With its cactus garden and fabulous view of the Pacific Ocean to inspire me, this beautiful flat situated right next to an ancient Spanish church seemed to be exactly the place I wanted. For such a large flat, the rent* seemed to be very reasonable. I told the real estate agent who was showing me the place, "I'll take it." After making a cash payment in advance, I was ready to settle in. Actually, I wanted to ask her a few questions about the area, but she seemed in such a hurry to get away, I didn't get the chance. So I was soon left alone in my temporary dream home.

I was blissfully happy*. Looking out on the sunny patio, I thought, "This is the REAL Mexico of my dreams." How real it was, I soon found out when the neighboring ancient church, which I had so admired, started loudly letting me know that it was 12 o'clock with the aid of* its church bells BOOMING into my room. They sounded ten times louder than the chimes of Big Ben in London!

In fact, the problem was worse than that of the Bali mosque, where I only had to endure* the sound of the azans five times a day. The church's bells would be echoing around my neighborhood on the hour every hour, 24 times a day! No wonder* the real estate agent was in a hurry to get away. She knew I would never take that room once I had heard those bells. When I called her to try and cancel the deal, she said that the policy of her company made

that impossible and added knowingly, "You should look before you leap*." I think she had used that English saying on many other clients who paid for that room and then, after being deafened by the church bells*, found out that there was no way that they could get their money back.

Of course, I'm sure that many devout Muslims and Christians enjoy these loud "religious" sounds echoing from minarets and churches, but in general I most certainly don't. As they say, "One man's meat is another man's poison"—especially when it comes to religious customs.

"Plastic Changed My Life!"

These are the words of Upi Hariwati, an Indonesian housewife, and she's NOT referring to plastic surgery*.

No, she's talking about her career as a saleslady for the giant US company Tupperware*, which manufactures* all kinds of plastic containers*, plates, boxes, bowls, etc. for household use. Aside from* the US, Indonesia is now Tupperware's biggest market. It's kind of a surprise because their products, while sturdy* and attractive, are not particularly cheap, especially for Indonesia where the daily wages* are often well under 10 US dollars*. However, the rising middle class and even families in the country find a very practical use for the Tupperware products they learn about at demonstration parties.

Upi Hariwati, a Tupperware sales agent, said selling the products was very difficult for her at first, as she had to walk the streets making presentations door-to-door. But after only two years, the unthinkable* has happened. From living in poverty all her life, she now has her own car to carry out business and has bought her own spacious house with money from the sales commissions* on Tupperware products. She says she really enjoys the Tupperware demonstration parties that she holds in her own home. Such parties, called "arisan," are considered quite normal in Indonesia, where meetings of housewives to discuss children, cooking and household topics is a kind of tradition.

Another housewife, Dewi, says the sales job has made her happier and more confident. Previously she was so shy that she could hardly say a word in conversations, even with her own family. Apart from shopping, she hardly ever went out of the house. She was a real "stay-at-home" girl who tried to hide her uneasiness as best she could. Now she is a different woman. Sometimes she even likes to shock her party guests. For example, usually one housewife will say, "It's true that Tupperware is beautiful, but it looks so fragile*. My kids will break it in no time." At that point Dewi may pick up a particularly delicate-looking container and smash it to the floor*, to the horror of her guests. She then picks it up off the floor and shows them that there's not even a scratch* on it. She may finish with the remark, "So you see, it's so strong that not even the naughtiest boy can break it. It's childproof*."

Looking back on her past, Dewi recalls that the financial condition of her family was so dire* that she knew she had to do something. When a friend introduced her to the Tupperware sales program, she refused the position at first, but eventually she forced herself to do it for the sake of* her family. To her surprise, she found she was quite successful at selling the products. As they say, "You never know what you can do until you try." So instead of being a "stay-at-home" girl, she turned into* a confident saleslady with many friends. Even her conservative Muslim husband, who had been resolutely against her joining Tupperware, said, "Wow! I've got a new kind of beautiful wife, and she's richer than me."

In fact, Tupperware now has around 250,000 salesladies around Indonesia, who have created new, confident, prosperous lives doing something they thought they never could. By the way, if you think I am being paid by Tupperware to write this, you are wrong. I just thought it would be interesting to show how a commonplace* American product can improve the lives of many thousands of Asian ladies in a dramatic way.

Also, I've written this story because it reminds me so much of my own experience in the US. After my graduation, I got a job as an account executive* with a large London advertising agency. After some time, to further my ambition* in the advertising field, I went to New York, which was then considered "the Vatican of advertising*." With my advertising experience, I thought that some 'lucky' ad agency there would eagerly employ me. How wrong I was! I was shown around beautiful agencies and invited to lunches in the best restaurants—but no job! Then I saw an advertisement in one of the big daily newspapers that reads, "Public relations

representative for publisher needed to distribute free cooking books, medical guides and Bibles, etc. to households prior to* publication." I thought, "Well that's something I CAN do. Everybody likes something free." So I went to a nicely furnished office and was shown all their beautiful books bound in imitation leather. I was told by an executive of Progress Research—for that was the name of the company—that all I had to do was to give out FREE copies of these books to middle-class families. In return, all they had to do was to give their opinion about these beautiful books before they were put on sale. I was offered the job almost immediately, but I demurred*. It seemed that SOMETHING was not quite right! I told the executive that I wanted time to think it over. The executive snapped back*, "You must decide now. You can see 20 other guys waiting in the reception who want this job. So take it or leave it NOW*!" Not much choice, so I took the job.

A secretary gave me a Greyhound* bus ticket to St Louis where, I was told, the Progress Research 'training school' was situated. The training school turned out to be a room in quite a nice hotel. And this was where I learned the exact truth about my job. Yes, it was true that households would receive free books BUT—and this was the problem—they also had to subscribe for THREE years to FOUR magazines if they wanted to receive these wonderful books! In other words, the REAL job was selling magazines on a door-to-door basis*. Many might say that this was one of the jobs on the lowest rung* of the "employment totem pole*." But I had to accept it because I had no money and Progress Research seemed to offer free accommodations and food. At least I thought so at that time.

So after memorizing a sales talk word-for-word, and arming myself with a sales kit* that included free books and volumes of information on the magazines I was selling, I started banging* on doors, but few were opened to me. The usual response of the householder was, "So you're selling magazines? I don't want any. Goodbye." The door would then be slammed* in my face. After a week of this, I just couldn't stand any more*. I told the CEO* of Progress Research I was leaving. He replied, "That's OK, but don't forget to pay us $600 for food and accommodations." When I explained that I thought that the food and board were provided free by his company and that anyway I had no money to pay him, his reaction was very negative: "You just go out on the street again and damn well* sell magazines until you CAN pay me the money you owe me. What do you think we are? A charity organization*?"

You may not believe it, but that was the best advice I ever had. They say, "A hungry salesman is the best salesman". It's true. When

I went on the street again, I was determined to succeed. Not only did I get into houses, I also started selling. It was just a wonderful feeling! When householders began telling me they agreed that the combination of a valuable book and magazine subscriptions was a really good deal, I gained confidence and success. I was REALLY selling successfully! Yes, like the Indonesian housewife I gained true confidence in myself, which was more important than the money I made. Frankly, it was not the ideal job, so after six months I quit, but I had saved enough to return to England and buy a car. On top of that*, it was a great experience from which I probably learned more about selling and human nature* than if I had studied for five years at a business college. As they say, "If at first you don't succeed, Try, Try, and TRY again."

From Dog Meat to Crufts Champion

"Miracle" is the name of an amazing mongrel* dog, because he IS a miracle. Originally, he was just another stray*, half-starved, diseased dog, sniffing for scraps* on a beach in Thailand. Later, however, he became a champion at the world-famous Crufts Dog Show* in Birmingham. How did this seemingly impossible transformation take place*?

If he had just stayed on that beach in Thailand, our miraculous hero's expected lifespan* would have been very short. It was on its way to becoming even shorter when he was caught by professional dog hunters, who planned to sell his body to a restaurant in Hanoi, Vietnam, where local gourmets relish the thought of eating 'dog meat stew.'* In fact, it is said that Vietnamese will eat ANYTHING on four legs except for chairs! I think it's true, because when I was there I saw snakes, lizards, bear paws*, and various horrible-looking unknown creatures preserved in glass jars ready to be eaten.

Anyway, that was what the dog hunters wanted to do with* Miracle, when they cruelly slung* his body into the back of a truck. Luckily for him, however, a member of the Phuket-based Soi Dog Foundation*, which takes care of abandoned* dogs, just happened to walk by the spot where the truck was parked. She took a flash photo of* what she thought were bodies of dead dogs. The flash of the camera made Miracle open his eyes, and he tried to escape from the truck. The lady with the camera saw this and shouted, "That dog's alive. Give him to me and I'll save him." Yes, the camera flash is what saved Miracle's life! The dog hunter tried to explain that the dog was so sick that he would die anyway, so what would be the use of taking him?

The lady answered, "Don't worry, we'll nurse him back to health*." And she was quite right. After several months of care and nursing at the Soi Dog Foundation, Miracle recovered* his health. He was a very handsome-looking dog, so the Foundation posted his picture on their Facebook* advertising, hoping that some dog lover would adopt* him.

It so happened that a Mrs. Leask from Scotland saw the photo on Facebook. She thought Miracle might be a good companion for her six-year-old son, Kyle, who was suffering from a severe case of autism*. It was true that she had adopted other dogs from Romania and Thailand for this purpose, but somehow Kyle just didn't take to* them. It was tragic that Kyle couldn't communicate with his parents or anyone in any way except to cry out when he felt frustrated, which was quite often. Indeed, he led a sad and solitary existence*.

However, as soon as Miracle entered the house, the atmosphere changed. Kyle and Miracle seemed to establish a close bond with each other immediately. It amazed everybody when they saw how well the two got on together.

Mrs. Leask talked about their relationship to the media, saying, "Kyle and Miracle have both faced so much hardship in their lives that there's an unspoken language between them, which only they can understand. When Kyle gets upset because he can't communicate what he wants to, Miracle will go and lie at his side for Kyle to touch and stroke* him. Kyle immediately calms down. It's amazing, but Miracle seems to automatically know when Kyle needs him. If Kyle simply wants some attention, Miracle will go over and shower him with kisses*. And it works the other way too. Kids can build up confidence in dogs where they seek solace*, and Miracle gets this in abundance* from Kyle."

It seems that Miracle had become very healthy, but was still nervous and sometimes moody due to his hard times on the beach. Now in his new home, he became a much happier dog. In a sense, Miracle received as much healing attention from Kyle as Kyle received from him. It was a 'two-way street.'

When someone suggested that they enter Miracle as a contestant* in the world-famous Crufts Dog Show, Mrs. Leask was very amused. She supposed that since Miracle was just a mongrel, he couldn't possibly compete against so many highly trained dogs with pedigrees going back years*. Then she learned that there was a 'Crufts Friends for Life' award*, which was given to dogs whose bravery, companionship and affection had supported their mainly handicapped owners in many remarkable ways. Pedigree didn't count at all.

Without many expectations of success—there were over 200 other dogs to compete with in this category—Mrs. Leask entered Miracle in the competition. She was very excited when Miracle was chosen, after a lot of competitive formalities*, to be among the four finalists*. More amazingly, Miracle was finally chosen by public vote to be the Crufts winner! Who could believe that a stray, diseased dog on a Thai beach could turn out to be a Crufts champion? But Miracle had proved that "A friend in need is a friend indeed.*" He had been a good friend to Kyle, who had also been a good friend to him. They both really needed each other. I think this is just a wonderful child and animal story.

Of course, trained dogs have many uses*. One of the most important uses is to sniff out drugs when people try to smuggle* them into the country illegally. Because of this, I had a

rather unpleasant experience at an airport in Ecuador. I had had a wonderful holiday in that colorful country, touring the Galapagos Islands on a yacht, boating down the Amazon, and doing some strenuous* hiking in the Andes Mountains. I was just about to leave by air for Cuba, my next holiday destination, when there was an announcement to the passengers on my plane, which was about to take off. We were all ordered to leave the plane, stand in line on the tarmac* with our hand baggage in front of us, and wait there in the hot sunshine. At last, two men with Alsatian dogs* appeared. What was happening? We soon found out, when the dogs started sniffing at all the hand baggage on the tarmac in front of us. They were looking for drugs. I later learned that it was quite common for drugs to be smuggled from Ecuador to Cuba and thence to Miami*. Well, I thought, I had nothing to fear ... until one of the dogs seemed to take a great interest in my shoulder bag. I wanted him just to go away and start sniffing the next person's bag, but he didn't. He just kept sniffing and sniffing at mine. Why?

The airport official asked me to follow him to a small office. There they roughly emptied out* all the things from my bag and thoroughly searched me. It was most unpleasant. I thought they might even PLANT drugs on me*. That happens sometimes in developing countries, as catching a drug smuggler may lead to a promotion. To their disappointment they found NOTHING. Well, at least they apologized and explained that some tablets I was carrying for high blood pressure might have been the reason for the dog's interest. As I entered the plane after some time, the passengers looked at me as if I WAS some kind of criminal. They say that, like Miracle, "A dog is man's best friend," but that sniffer dog was NO friend of mine!

Insect Burger, Anyone?

The very thought of eating an insect, even touching one*, is disgusting* to many people. Yet packaged "Insect Burger" is being sold in a certain country by a huge supermarket chain. Is it in Africa or Asia, where poorer people have been known to eat bugs* for generations? No, the packets of Insect Burger are being sold in Switzerland! They say the bugs used have been bred under very hygienic* Swiss conditions. The fact is,* gourmet dishes* using insects are now being served in upmarket* restaurants in London, Copenhagen, Berne, Bangkok and other major international cities. It's true that restaurant patrons* are not rushing in and shouting, "I MUST have an INSECT Burger!*" But they may do so once they get over* their negative attitude* toward such dishes.

For example, in Thailand, bugs were regularly eaten by poorer people in the North, but carefully eschewed* by the elite in Bangkok.

Now tastes are changing. Miss Rata Bussakornnun, a cosmetics executive based in Bangkok, was a bit nervous about trying insect cuisine in an upmarket restaurant called Backyard. Still, in the spirit of adventure she first ordered scallops topped with bamboo EARTHWORMS*, and followed that with fish in ANT sauce*. "Both dishes were delicious," she said without hesitation. "I've been won over.*" Also traditional *tsukudani* cuisine, which often includes locusts*, has been appreciated* for many years by Japanese gourmets.

Of course, the main problem with promoting insect dishes is not the taste of the insect itself, which can be quite delicious, but rather people's preconceptions*, their severely negative attitudes about eating bugs. I found this out for myself not with insects but with certain meats about which I had the wrong attitude.

One time, my host in a country town in the Philippines offered me a dish that I thought was homemade yakitori. I congratulated* him and told him that the chicken was really delicious. He laughed and told me, "Actually, it's not chicken. You've just eaten a RAT*!" I wanted to be sick when I heard that. Of course, it was the thought, not the meat, which made me feel that way. My host later explained that he had barbecued a clean, rice-eating rat from the countryside, not a dirty city rat, so I didn't have to worry. Still, for me a rat IS a rat, wherever it comes from*.

Another time in the Philippines I thought I'd really enjoyed a good beef stew ... until I saw the skull* of a DOG at the bottom of the huge pot used for cooking it. I was angry with my friend who had promised me it was Japanese beef. "Yes," he responded, "but if I'd told you it was dog meat, you wouldn't have eaten it." It's true that he told me a 'white lie*,' but he does have a point*; there was nothing wrong with the meat. It was my ATTITUDE that was wrong.

A similar incident* happened to me in Kuantan, Malaysia. I'd just finished an absolutely delicious but expensive dish of lobster thermidor*, and I complimented* the chef. He told me it was his signature dish*, but that he himself never touched lobster. I was

Locust tsukudani or Wormburger?

surprised and asked why. He replied, "Here in Kuantan, we think of lobster as a 'dirty dish.' After all, when you think of it, lobsters are just the scavengers* of the deep, picking up any old rubbish* from the bottom of the ocean, so they must be dirty. We used to give lobsters to prisoners. Now we give lobsters to TOURISTS, and we can't believe the high prices they pay for them." Anyway, I think I had the right attitude in this case.

But can we influence not only the elite but also ordinary people, so that everyone enjoys ingesting* insects in the same way many of us enjoy eating lobster now? Perhaps it's possible. After all, they said you could NEVER stop people smoking cigarettes. Now after a vigorous* non-smoking campaign, most people HAVE stopped. Can we do the same for dietary habits*?

It's a more important question than you may think. By 2050, it is reckoned*, the world population will be around 10 billion. How CAN we feed so many? It seems that the traditional methods of food production such as breeding cattle and planting crops will not produce nearly enough food to satisfy such a huge population. Even now, families living in poor areas with several children seem to be half-starving*, because they cannot afford a balanced diet! For them and us, a diet of insects may be the answer.

It is estimated that for each human being on this planet, there are 40 tons of insects! In addition, there are 1,900 edible* species of 'bugs,' including grasshoppers, ants, beetles, spiders, worms, and larvae*. In fact, there's no shortage of nutrition*. Insects are quite healthy to eat because they contain protein, calcium, iron and most of the essential vitamins we need. Moreover, they have almost no fat or cholesterol. So, whether you're starving or overweight, the insect diet* is a bonus*.

Since rich people in ancient Rome and Greece used to eat insects, why don't we*, who need them more? Bugs are cheap and easy to breed, so they present a good chance for businesses to make big profits. With the right marketing, insect breeding could benefit the whole world. Right now, Thailand is leading the way by breeding bamboo worms or larvae in farms around the country, because they've become a popular dish even among the elite. Bamboo Earthworm Vodka* is also a hit. It's made by steeping* worms in the liquor for a long time.

Sometimes it's difficult to find a present for a rich friend "who's got everything." Why not try giving him a bottle of Earthworm Vodka? It's unlikely that he's got that!

Will Elephants Completely Disappear in 20 Years' Time?

Just recently, young people have been demonstrating all over the world against the indiscriminate* killing of wild animals in Africa, especially elephants and rhinos*. As you may know, elephants are killed for their ivory tusks*, and rhinos are murdered for their horns*. You may think 'murdered' is too strong a word for this situation, but I don't think so. Premeditated* killing for profit is murder.

It may shock you to know that if the murders of these magnificent animals continue at the present rate, soon there may be no elephants or rhinos left in the world. It is estimated that in 20 years, elephants and rhinos may actually become extinct*, just as dinosaurs* did ages ago. For example, 30 years ago, 170,000 elephants freely roamed the jungles of Kenya. There was no protection, because it wasn't needed. Now there are less than 30,000 elephants, and although they are kept in highly protected reservations*, their numbers are dwindling* rapidly. It is reckoned that in Africa, 35,000 elephants and 1,100 rare rhinos are killed every year by local poachers*, who use high-powered rifles, helicopters and advanced communication equipment to follow and kill their prey. Once spotted*, these poor animals have almost no chance of survival. Meanwhile*, it's very difficult, almost impossible, to catch the poachers, who disappear long before the wildlife police arrive.

The buying and selling of ivory tusks and rhino horns is considered by international criminal gangs* to be a lucrative* business that brings in billions of dollars a year. So where do the ivory tusks end up? Newly rich Chinese millionaires are believed to be the main buyers. They will pay huge sums of money for ivory carvings* and for rhino horns used in traditional medicine or as aphrodisiacs*. One naive* Chinese tourist was asked why he came to Africa. He replied, "My daughter is dying of cancer. The doctor told me that consuming powdered rhino horn would save her life. I can't get it in China, so that's why I've come to

Will this be a school class in 2050?

Africa. I'll pay any amount of money to get it." I am sure he will, but it won't do his daughter any good*. Chinese are very clever at most things, but when it comes to medicines they have crazy theories*. Rhino horns have no more healing properties* than fingernails or the hooves* of horses; the latter have almost the same composition but, of course, are much cheaper. I remember entering a Chinese medicine shop in Hong Kong just out of curiosity*. The bodies and dried parts of many rare animals were for sale, including those of bears, bats, foxes, seahorses*, sharks, lions, tigers—the list goes on and on. The prize exhibit* in a glass case was a dried piece of flesh* about 12 centimeters long, which was selling for $1,800. "What can THAT be?" I asked the salesman. "It's a genuine tiger's penis," he said proudly. "It's the world's best aphrodisiac." Well, I'd rather put my money on Viagra* to do the trick, since it's much cheaper. But having tried neither, I may be wrong!

One time when I was in South Africa, I went on a safari trip in Kruger National Park, which was a wonderful experience. Seeing wild animals in their natural habitat is something I shall never forget. However, we also saw something very horrible, too, which was also unforgettable. It was the body of an elephant lying on the ground. It was such a pitiful sight. It seems she had bled to death* after being shot and having her ivory tusks sawn off* by evil poachers. We couldn't go near, as the 'murder scene' had been fenced off* for investigative purposes. Our safari guide told us that the poachers were probably from Mozambique. The border was nearby, so the poachers could just cross the border with their booty*, making it difficult for South African authorities to pursue or prosecute* them. Our guide also told us that the bodies of poachers were sometimes found in the huge park. Maybe the poachers had died because they had lost their way or been attacked by lions. And perhaps they deserved their fate.

Even now, millionaires and celebrities can pay $20,000 or up to go hunting and come back with such trophies as a tusk or a rhino horn. It's not a good idea. For example, the King of Spain went hunting elephants with his girlfriend. That was a particularly BAD idea, since most Spaniards* were suffering hard times, with almost 30% of young people unemployed. Shortly after that, His Majesty* had to abdicate in favor of* his son. Now he's an 'ex-King*.' Well, perhaps that was the elephants' revenge.

The UK's royal family is very concerned for Africa's wildlife, but there is allegedly a difference of opinion between Prince William and his father, Prince Charles. Prince William thinks ALL ivory objects must be destroyed, including old carvings. Prince Charles, who has an extensive collection of antique carvings, doesn't think so, because he feels certain objects represent Japanese art at its best. It's not often I agree with Prince Charles, but I do so in this case, as I have a few exquisite netsuke* myself. I want to keep them, but I won't buy any more in the future.

Of course, at one time it was thought that tuna was an endangered species. Lovers of Japanese cuisine were faced with the nightmare of tuna sushi and sashimi vanishing from their dining tables. But no more. Using tuna eggs, it may now be possible to breed* enough tuna to satisfy the sashimi and sushi markets. One day it might be possible to breed elephants and rhinos in the same way. Perhaps the clever Chinese can manage to do this. Then they will be able to just harvest* the horns and the tusks, which regrow over time. Instead of killing these magnificent animals, they will just need to give them a 'haircut.'

Why Does "Affluenza*" Help Millionaire Killers?

Fairly recently Ethan Couch, a spoiled 16-year-old son of wealthy* parents, was finally sentenced to* just two years in prison for needlessly killing four people and seriously injuring some others in a frightful* traffic accident for which he was 100% to blame. Many wonder whether this light sentence was because he was young or because he came from a rich family. When you study the history of this case, you will see it was probably because of the latter reason. It is said that wealthy people in Texas can get away with murder*, thanks to their clever, expensive defense attorneys*. People who are poor and non-white can expect a long prison sentence if they can't afford a good attorney.

Just after the accident, it seemed that Couch would get away with doing no prison time at all for his lethal carelessness*. During his first trial, his defense attorney argued that it would be wrong to put this young criminal in prison, because he was suffering from "affluenza." Affluenza? What can that be? According to his attorney, Couch was so affluent and young that he didn't understand the consequences of his bad actions. In other words, he thought that his parents were so affluent that they could even buy his way out of punishment for criminal activities. Due to this state of mind*, he was not really responsible for the shocking consequences of his crime. It was all because of his severe case of affluenza.

Previously, no one had ever heard of affluenza as an excuse for criminal conduct*. Even in legal circles*, it sounded unbelievable. But somehow Couch's brilliant, high-priced lawyer made it sound quite credible to the Texas judge and jury*. Perhaps they didn't fully understand the circumstances of what had happened. An abusive childhood* could conceivably* provide a mitigating* defense for later criminal activities, but in a case like this, where a rich criminal has had all the advantages of a good home, education, and loving parents, the sentence for the taking of human life—even by carelessness—ought to* be longer, not shorter. Couch should already have realized that with great wealth comes social responsibility*.

Immediately before he started his deadly* journey on the road, Couch had stolen two cases of beer from a store, as recorded by surveillance cameras. Once in his father's Ford pickup truck, he raced along the highway at 110 kilometers an hour in a 64-kilometer-an-hour speed zone with seven young passengers, most of whom ended up in the hospital*. Two hours after the accident, he was tested for alcohol and drugs. Not only did he have three times the legal limit of alcohol in his blood*, he also tested positive for marijuana and Valium*. Quite a combination* for a 16-year-old!

When police looked into Couch's criminal record, they found he had been cautioned* by police just the previous year, when he had been found drunk in his car with a naked 14-year-old girl and an empty bottle of vodka by his side! There was no real investigation to see whether he had done anything wrong with this underage* girl, and so he was let off with a caution* instead of being arrested. If he had been arrested, he would have done time in a juvenile institution* and undergone appropriate therapy. At the end of it, he might have realized he had social responsibilities, including careful driving; and that could have meant that the lives of four people would have been saved. Yes, he should have been imprisoned at that time. No doubt* his parents' money saved him from having to serve a custodial sentence*. The whole affair probably demonstrated to young Couch that money could buy anything. So yes, it was also a case of affluenza, which means he was not responsible, right? I don't think so.

In fact, he was very much responsible both then and later when he drove drunk. He plowed into* a group of people who were standing by the side of the road waiting for help because their car had stalled*. There was absolutely NO excuse for what Couch did.

Anyway, it seems that Judge Jean Boyd, who presided over* Couch's first trial, agreed with this crazy affluenza defense. She only sentenced him to 10-year probation*, which included time in a luxurious rehabilitation home*. Couch was to serve NO prison time at all for killing four people! And yet, inexplicably, 10 years earlier Judge Boyd had sentenced a poor boy, Eric Miller, to a tough 20 years in prison for a similar offense*. Miller was the same age as Couch and was involved in an almost identical accident, killing only one person. But he didn't get probation; he got 20 years in prison! At the time, the judge admitted that the severe abuse Miller suffered in childhood could have been considered a mitigating factor, but she threw the book at him* anyway. So WHY the difference in sentences? Was it because Couch was rich and Miller was poor? The victims of Couch's killing spree* were outraged by his "slap-on-the-wrist*" punishment, as were many others. Of course, Couch was a teenager, but he probably figured that his age and his family's wealth would protect him from consequences. Quite a few psychologists* nowadays say that teenagers think and act like adults, so they should be accountable as adults. Instead, many youngsters who do something wrong can say,

The charge is the same, but the sentence is very different.

"You can't touch me. I'm UNDERAGE."

You would think that his mother, Mrs. Couch, would be thankful for such a light sentence and would willingly comply with the court's conditions of probation and rehabilitation, which could certainly have been of great help to her son. Not at all. It seems she was a "mother from hell*." She and her son packed their bags and absconded* to Mexico, where they probably thought they would be beyond the reach of US law*. They were wrong. Soon they were recognized staying in a modest hotel in Puerto Vallarta. They were extradited* by the Mexican authorities and put under arrest when they landed separately in Texas.

As previously mentioned, in his second trial Ethan Couch was finally sentenced to two years in prison, but only two years. Nowadays, with the bad policy of going light on criminals, this may be reduced to one year for "good behavior." It seems that in the States and Europe, the victims of violent crimes never seem to get the justice they deserve. If Couch gets out of prison so soon, I wouldn't be surprised if he ends up killing still more people with his drunken, reckless driving. Why should he care when he can always plead "Not guilty,"* on account of* affluenza?

Did a Ray of Sunshine* Reveal Dark Secrets?

Most people welcome a ray of sunshine. It makes them feel happy and relaxed. But this was NOT the case with General Prawit Wongsuwan, the Deputy Prime Minister of Thailand. Just one ray of sunshine made him feel very unhappy and stressed out*. What was the cause of such a strange reaction?

Well, Prawit was sitting in the front row of a newly reshuffled cabinet*, posing for a photo, when a dazzling ray of sunshine hit his face. He put up his hand to shield his eyes from the light. When he did so, his cuff pulled back to reveal a very, very expensive Richard Mille watch on his wrist and a brilliant four-carat diamond ring on his finger. Cameras around him began clicking*, and the sunlit* luxuries found their way into the news*. After enlarged photos were carefully examined, the shiny objects were alleged to be worth around $500,000.

You might think, "So what? That's his business." Of course, if Prawit had just been a successful businessman, there would have been no fuss*; but he became a career politician after retiring from the army. As such, he has a duty to publicly declare all personal assets above the value of $7,500, and the precious assets on his wrist and finger had NOT been declared.

Some insisted that such an oversight shouldn't matter much and that the huge amount of publicity generated in unsympathetic news stories was just "making a mountain out of a molehill."* Others claimed that the purchase of such undeclared luxuries suggested corruption*. I don't think so. But later the Deputy Prime Minister showed journalists his Seiko watch, which was valued at a measly* $8,000 and HAD been legally declared. In any case, most of us tourists like the present government, as it has brought peace to Bangkok—so welcome after the raging battles* that took place just outside our hotel lobbies not so long ago.

Frankly, I don't know why some people need to spend thousands of dollars on watches, except to show off how rich they are. A Luminox watch that I bought several years ago for less than $300 still keeps perfect time*, even when I'm diving underwater. I think a lot of famous Swiss watch brands spend more money on expensive advertising than on the watches themselves. Still, I don't believe owning an expensive Swiss watch is a sign of corruption.

To change the subject, Tanzania faces a bigger problem than stamping out* corruption—stamping out TB (tuberculosis)*, a disease that kills hundreds of thousands of people every year in Africa. According to WHO (World Health Organization), TB killed more than 1.7 million people worldwide in 2016. It spreads so quickly because it's a highly infectious disease*. The trouble is, diagnosis* is slow and expensive. It takes four days for trained chemists* to screen* 100 samples of mucus* that they suspect may contain TB germs.

Now they've discovered a new method of screening, not by chemists but by rats. Yes, RATS! You may not believe it, but specially trained African pouched rats* can detect TB in 100 samples in only 20 minutes, not four days. According to Apopo, a Belgian charity that is sponsoring* the use of these 30-centimeter-long rats, the results are close to 100% accurate. It makes sense.* Dogs and even pigs can sniff out* illegal drugs in smugglers' baggage, so why shouldn't rats be able to use their olfactory* abilities to sniff out TB in mucus? If it's true, then millions of lives in Africa might be saved. And the rats don't need watches or diamonds as a reward—a big piece of cheese will do*.

Did the Dangerous Alligator Need "Anger Management*"?

They say that animals and humans may suffer from sudden bouts of anger* for no particular reason, and that this condition, at least in humans, can be controlled through anger management therapy*.

If it were available to animals, such therapy might have benefited a certain alligator* in Florida, because his anger turned out to be very unfortunate for both himself and Matthew Riggins. As the story begins, 22-year-old Matthew needed money rather quickly to take his girlfriend out to a fancy restaurant. The only way he could think of to get the money was to rob* one of the big houses situated nearby. With this in mind, he donned* black clothes like a ninja, so he wouldn't be seen, and started to case* the houses to choose one he could break into. Unfortunately for him, a local resident noticed him acting suspiciously. The resident called the police on his mobile*, and they responded very quickly. When Matthew saw the police searching the area for him, he tried to hide by diving into* a nearby pond. He was never seen again. His girlfriend, who was expecting to meet him later that evening, tried calling him on his mobile, but there was no answer. It was most mysterious. WHAT had happened to him?

What Matthew didn't know when he dived into the dark pond was that a fierce alligator lived there. The gator regarded the pond as HIS territory, and intruders* made him very, very angry. Perhaps if he had undergone "anger management" therapy, he wouldn't have been so angry, but he certainly was when he saw somebody dive into his pond. And so he attacked and killed poor Matthew. Later on, after a lot of searching, investigators found out what happened. They were able to capture that angry alligator* and open up his stomach, where they identified* some of Matthew's anatomy* through DNA* analysis. Most of his body, which was found later, had hardly been touched. The authorities believe that Matthew was attacked because of the alligator's anger, not because he needed a meal.

Actually, the alligator population is expanding so rapidly in Florida that they pose a great danger to people living near the swamps*. Alligators have been found on golf courses, in gardens, and even in houses when garden doors have been left open. I remember some time ago I was on a small tourist boat for an "Everglades Tour*" in that area. The highlight of the tour was advertised as, "A wrestler fighting with a man-eating alligator." Yes, we saw a huge alligator who seemed happy just lying asleep on a patch of grass* by the water. Soon the wrestler approached him for the great fight, but the alligator wanted none of it. He just ran into the water. The wrestler hauled him back by his tail*, but the alligator just ran back into the water. Finally, with apparent reluctance* the alligator engaged his opponent in a strange kind of wrestling match*, until the wrestler was able to proclaim victory by holding the poor creature still with his back on the grass*. After being rewarded with a big chunk of meat*, the gator was allowed to return to the water and swim away. We all clapped* but wondered whether the alligator was trained to always swim back for another exhibition*—and another big chunk of meat!

One of my most interesting experiences in Thailand was a visit to the Tiger Temple, not to wrestle with the tigers but to meet them. It's a remarkable sensation to wander around tigers who are just lying around in the open and not behind bars. Once you overcome initial fears, you can sit by them, stroke them and even "take a selfie*" to show you cuddling up to* your tiger friend. The Buddhist monks who look after them claim that because of their gentle treatment, no one has ever been attacked by a tiger. They absolutely deny that the tigers have ever been given drugs. They do look rather sleepy, but I guess it's the hot weather.

Getting back to the subject of anger management, one of my friends spent three months in a Thai Buddhist monastery* trying to overcome her 'anger problem' through meditation. It's strange, because usually she's kind, generous and calm, but then for seemingly no reason at all, she "flies off the handle*" with anger. So did the Buddhist monastery cure her of her sudden outbursts*? No, it didn't. In fact, the size of the 'donation' that the monks requested from her made her angrier than ever! She was even angrier than when Harrods department store in London demanded 2 pounds ($3) for services in the ladies' comfort room*. That kind of service is free in the States, but Harrods IS an expensive store. Well, you can't please everybody.*

Another animal story often featured in the media concerns an elephant called Hanako, who has been living at Inokashira Park Zoo in Tokyo. Certainly, she doesn't need anger management therapy, but since she has lived all alone in the zoo for the last 61 years, many people think she's sad and depressed. Her story has been widely publicized in Thailand, her original home. Many years ago, Captain Somwang Sarasas sent Hanako by sea at his own expense to the Ueno Zoo. At that time, there were no elephants in Japan, and so he thought Japanese children would love to see Hanako. Yes, they were thrilled, but Hanako may not have been so excited about it. She's existed all by herself in a cold concrete

Lonely Hanako

enclosure with no bare earth*, grass or trees. Her zookeepers claim she's quite content, as the many Japanese volunteers who look after her are her friends. Hanako gets special food, including expensive peeled Cavendish bananas, as she has a weak digestive system*. Of course, it's nice she has so many human friends, but they are NOT elephants, which I'm sure she would prefer, as elephants are extremely social animals enjoying each other's company. Actually, 206,000 Thai and Japanese people have signed an online petition* requesting that she be moved into the company of other elephants. Of course, in a sense she's "an old

Miss," the oldest elephant in Japan, so I don't know how she would adapt to the company of younger elephants who, in their world, are mostly "teenagers."

Sometimes we forget that animals also have complex feelings ranging from rage and happiness to depression and loneliness*. We should really think about how they feel, especially when they are dependent on us for their existence.

It's More Fun in the Philippines ... with Lots of Money!

It seems that there are not so many bank holdups* nowadays. Well, why should there be, when just by pressing the right computer keys, you can steal millions with almost no risk?

That's exactly the kind of theft that happened at the Federal Reserve Bank of New York*. Hackers* broke into the bank's computers, stealing a whopping* 81 million dollars that was part of Bangladesh's foreign reserves*. Maybe it was one of the biggest bank robberies* in history and, sadder still, it was one of the world's poorest countries that took the hit*.

But in one sense Bangladesh was lucky, because the hackers could have stolen more, much more*. The cyber thieves actually tried to steal almost a billion dollars by feeding a demand* for $951,000,000 into the computer. But as luck would have it*, a nervous clerk made a small mistake when typing in the details of the illegal transfer*. He should have typed Shalika "Foundation" in the request, but he actually typed Shalika "Faundation." Fortunately, an alert* clerk in Deutsche Bank noticed the misspelling, so the huge transaction was stopped by the appropriate authorities. The misspelling seems to have been a small mistake, but it ended up having very positive consequences*. The theft could have drained* a huge part of Bangladesh's foreign reserves. However, the cancellation* order didn't stop the theft of 81 million dollars, which had already been processed*.

So how was it possible to breach the security* of such an important bank? It's still a mystery. Some claim that Chinese thieves were behind the clever, well-prepared operation, that they used "malware," or malicious* software, to break into the bank's computer system after stalking* and analyzing it for two weeks. Whoever did it somehow installed the malware into the Federal Reserve Bank of New York's computer system. Maybe they had seen the tourist advertising slogan, "It's More Fun in the

Philippines," because the Philippines was where they decided to transmit the money*, using Rizal Commercial Banking Corporation in Manila as the place to deposit their ill-gotten wealth*. Maia Deguito, the manager of this bank, is alleged to have given the thieves her full cooperation*. It seems that without the usual checking, she granted permission for four accounts with fictitious names* to be set up, and the money was deposited in these. When the theft came to light* and an attempt was made to freeze the accounts*, authorities were told, "It's too late. The money's gone!"

Critics of the bank claim that it DID have time to freeze the money. In any case, Ms. Deguito's movements certainly weren't frozen, as she was detained* just as she was about to board a plane leaving Manila. Also one of Ms. Deguito's subordinates testified* that he saw her put a large package into the back of her car and it was NOT a Chinese restaurant take-away*. It was a financial take-away containing 20 million pesos (about $430,000)!

So far Ms. Deguito hasn't said much. When called upon to* publicly testify before a committee, she answered, "I can't say anything because of self-incrimination*." On another occasion, she said she had to remain silent because of "bank secrecy." All this silence is a "red flag*" indicating that she may have been involved in the theft. However, she has hinted that even if she has done wrong, there are many mysterious "higher-ups*" who are still more deeply involved.

So, how could 81 million dollars just disappear into thin air*? Nobody seems to know where this huge sum of money has ended up—or if they do, they are not saying. After some investigation, it was found that the money had been transmitted to four of the huge casinos that have been constructed along Manila Bay. It can rightly be said that these palatial* casinos are ideal for "money laundering*," because unlike other businesses in the Philippines, they are exempt from* financial investigation. That, together with the Philippines' strict bank secrecy laws, makes the casinos a money launderer's paradise.

By the way, "money laundering" doesn't mean washing the bank notes with soap, but using various means to change illegally gained "dirty" money into legally gained "clean" cash. I've never done it myself, because all my money is hard-earned and very, very clean—what there is of it*! Anyway, it is alleged that soon after the transfer the money was exchanged for gambling chips, which were then converted* to currencies of the thieves' choosing. But because of the Philippine secrecy laws, which some politicians hope to change, it has been difficult to trace the money. It all seems like a Hollywood movie plot, or perhaps a new version of the game of Monopoly*.

So people are asking about the identity of the Mr. Big* who orchestrated* and profited from this complicated theft. It is said that a Chinese-Filipino, Mr. Kim Wong, may be a key figure in the operation. Ms. Deguito claimed that he was the one who opened up the four fictitious bank accounts that received the money. Mr. Wong is a millionaire* "high roller*" operating several businesses, including casinos, but by the time he was asked to testify before a government committee, this prominent businessman had disappeared. It was claimed that he had suddenly gone to Hong Kong for "health reasons." No surprise there. When politicians or businessmen engaged in "monkey business"* are asked to account for* their actions, they often take off somewhere for "health reasons." They may take shelter* in hospitals with compliant* doctors, as Gloria Macapagal Arroyo*, a former president of the Philippines, was then doing. She, too, was apprehended* as she was about to board a plane at Manila Airport. But why should so many people be trying to leave the Philippines when it's so much more "fun" to be there? Mr. Wong must have faced an emergency, especially as doctors are so expensive in Hong Kong. Perhaps he needed 81 million dollars to pay their exorbitant* fees.

Of course, casinos are fun. I was quite impressed as I toured one of these palatial gambling dens* and viewed the marble floors, the chandeliers, the gourmet restaurants, and the gaming tables. Everything necessary was there in that elegant ambience*—except for gamblers! There were so few of them that I wondered how the casinos made money. It

certainly was not from the residents of nearby Tondo, a slum where many people make less than $2 a day. Perhaps it's because the casinos operate a special kind of laundry! Anyway, one local gambler I spoke to said*, "The Philippines only used to be famous for fruit, but now we can be famous for fruit machines* too". Wow!

Well, this is the story so far, but I'm sure a lot more will be revealed in the future. I may have got some of the details wrong, as different newspapers have different versions. One media account has* Mr. Wong going to Singapore, while another says it was Hong Kong. I've just read that he's returned to the Philippines, so perhaps he's healthy again. Also, one version claims that the message's misspelling was "fandation," while another claims it was "faundation." "Faundation" sounds more likely. Anyway, talking about the characters involved, perhaps Ms. Deguito and Mr. Wong are just small cogs in a giant machinery* of corruption that includes high officials in the States, China, the Philippines, and Bangladesh. Perhaps they're all having fun somewhere in the Philippines with all that money! It's a pity that the poor people of the Philippines and Bangladesh can't share that fun with them. As I've said, this is not the end of the story, but it will be interesting and important to see how it all pans out*.

Are Cows Causing Climate Change*?

So much has been written about climate change and its causes. Motor vehicles, factories, and coal are always mentioned, and it's a fact that they do cause terrible pollution*. It's only going to get worse as China, India, and other developing countries concentrate on industrialization. But one source of pollution is hardly ever considered*, and I think it will really surprise you. It's cows!

Yes, cows with their methane-filled farts* are a major source of pollution, one of the main reasons why agriculture produces 18% of the world's greenhouse gases*, more than the total gases emitted* by motor vehicles. It is estimated that the production of one kilo of beef annually yields the equivalent of 34.6 kg of carbon dioxide*, compared with lamb's 17.4 kg and pork's 6.35 kg. Chicken, which is cheapest and healthiest, produces only 4.57 kg. So it's a good idea to consume chicken rather than beef or pork as part of your diet. But best of all* is a diet including insects. They are the least harmful to the world's atmosphere*, as almost no methane gas comes from insects.

Since the world population* of cows is now between 1.3 billion and 1.5 billion and growing, you can see that a huge amount of deadly gas is produced by their collective* farts. Also, it must be remembered that in the short term*, cow's methane gas is 28 times stronger than carbon dioxide, so you can understand how lethal it is.

But how is it that cute cows produce so much harmful gas? I'm sorry to say that it's not only through farting from the backside but also by burping* through the mouth. I think this negative characteristic is not publicly discussed much, because cows are such useful animals from which we obtain milk, leather, and mouth-watering steaks*. We really can't do without cows. Also cattle ranchers* would lose their jobs, not only in Texas and Australia but also in Japan, where the world's most delicious and most expensive steaks come from. Although ranchers outside of Japan have produced their versions of "Wagyu" beef, in my opinion, Matsuzaka marbled* beef continues to reign supreme*—if you can afford it and don't worry that you may be indirectly contributing to climate change. I have to admit that thinking about climate change doesn't spoil my appetite* for Japanese steaks!

Is anything being done about this problem of methane gas emanating* from cows? Yes, research is being carried out* in Denmark, Australia, the UK, and Africa. Scientists are discovering that a special kind of grass, which cows like to eat, might eliminate* the methane gas caused by ordinary grass. Also, some success has been found when cows digest seaweed*, which is healthy for humans, too. One experiment carried out during this research was quite imaginative. It involved putting large airtight plastic bubbles over cows*. This was designed to trap* the cow's gas in the bubble, which could then be used for generating electricity*. A good idea, but it turned out to be too expensive, and the cows didn't enjoy it either.

Surprisingly, religion plays quite a positive role regarding gas from cows and pigs. While

Muslims won't touch pork, because it's considered to be an unclean meat, Hindus won't eat beef, because cows are considered to be holy animals. For example, if a cow starts eating vegetables on sale along a city street, the seller is not allowed to stop this holy animal's consumption of his wares*. All he can do is to watch as the cow munches away* at his precious vegetables. Anyway, let's hope researchers find the right kind of grass to eliminate the harmful effect of cows' farts.

Now I would like to change the subject from cows to the use of one word in the previous paragraphs: "fart." It is NOT used in polite society*, as it is considered to be too vulgar*. A more polite term would be "to pass wind*," but I've used "fart" here because there is no alternative. It sounds funny if you say a cow is "passing wind." Such a polite expression is called a "euphemism*." It means a nice, pleasant word to disguise* something that might be considered vulgar or unpleasant. For instance, "maids" may like to be called "domestic helpers*." It's common in business to employ* euphemisms. For instance, it may be difficult, if you're a boss, to tell one of your workers that he's going to be fired or dismissed. It sounds more sympathetic to say, "I'm afraid we'll have to let you go.*" Sometimes you have to use a white lie*. Recently I called the CEO of a travel company, but I couldn't speak to him immediately. His secretary told me, "He can't speak to you now, because he's in the toilet." Well, that might have been true, but it would have been better if she had said, "I'm sorry, he's in conference now. Shall I have him call you back?"

The usage of "ethnic cleansing*" is also a euphemism that has often been used in recent news when describing the brutal actions of

Myanmar's soldiers against the minority Muslim Rohingyas. "Ethnic cleansing" doesn't really sound so bad. It sounds as if you're cleaning the bathroom. However, its actual meaning is very different. It means that an innocent and helpless minority people are being persecuted* through harassment, destruction of their homes, and even murder. Hitler described his murder of millions of Jews as "the final solution." Of course it was extreme ethnic cleansing, but that expression hadn't been invented in those days. On the whole, it's best not to use euphemisms. As they say, "Let's call a spade a spade*." But I think it's still better to say "pass wind" rather than "fart"— except when talking about research on cows.

Improve Your English with Shakespeare!

The 400th anniversary of the death of William Shakespeare on April 23, 1616, was marked* around the world. Scholars* speculate that he probably died at the age of 52 after a hard drinking session*. Perhaps if he had lived to 70, we could have enjoyed even more of his exciting plays, but we must be satisfied with the 38 plays and numerous sonnets that he left us.

Mozart died at a still younger age, 35. One wonders how much more glorious music he could have composed if he had lived longer. Although at least ten times more people are living on Earth at present and we are blessed with advanced technology, there is not one genius who even comes close to the creative output of Shakespeare or Mozart in terms of quality or quantity.

There's no question that Shakespeare is the greatest writer in the English language. The fact that his works have been translated into almost every language in the world suggests that he may be the greatest writer in ANY language. With this in mind, I have adopted a special "mini-essay" format for this month's contribution*. In each of the short statements that comprise this collection, I offer opinions on contemporary situations that include words (in CAPITAL letters) that originate with Shakespeare. Even now Shakespeare's sayings and quotations are used to express a point of view in colorful language. Nowadays so many English speakers use Shakespeare's words frequently without realizing that they began with the Bard*, who coined* them over 400 years ago.

1. For UK citizens, the Brexit* vote was a matter of whether TO BE, OR NOT TO BE*. (As for me, I voted to leave the EU, as it was a matter of whether the UK would be independent or not. I don't want us to be the slaves* of ignorant bureaucrats in Brussels.)

2. If millions more migrants enter the UK, THEY'LL EAT US OUT OF HOUSE AND HOME*. (That is, they'll use up all our resources, such as access to medical clinics,

schools, and hosts of other services. There won't be much left for the poor British taxpayers.)

3. At one sushi shop in Tokyo I ate *toro, uni, ika, ikura,* and *kohada*. IT WAS A DISH FIT FOR THE GODS*. (I use the Japanese names for the fish, since the sushi experience is as unique to Japan as kimono. Sure, sushi has gone global, but ONLY in Japan can you get the real thing at a counter.)

4. My secretary seemed angry when I complained that she was a few minutes late to work. IT'S BETTER TO BE THREE HOURS TOO SOON THAN ONE MINUTE TOO LATE*, I told her. I don't think she agreed with me— or with Shakespeare!

5. COME WHAT MAY*, I'll always love my wife. We'll never get divorced. (Whatever happens, good or bad, we'll continue in the same way. That's why we didn't need the prenuptial agreements* that many couples draw up nowadays.)

6. Everything seems rosy right now, but I think we're LIVING IN A FOOL'S PARADISE*. According to some forecasts, our investments may soon be worthless, and we'll

have nothing to live on. (Fools enjoy the comfort of temporary prosperity and success without considering that it may end very soon. Actually, I'm not quite so pessimistic.)

7. I told my son, "John, you spend 12 hours a day playing games online. Like other young people, you don't realize how dangerous computer addiction is to your mental and social life. If you want to graduate this year, IT'S HIGH TIME* you stopped playing games and started doing your homework." (It's necessary to take the right action NOW and not postpone it.)

8. I'm afraid I'm IN A PICKLE*. I gambled away all my money in Vegas and I don't have a way to get home. (To suddenly be experiencing extreme difficulties.)

9. Seeing that the visitors were nervous, the Queen BROKE THE ICE by cracking a joke*. Everyone relaxed and realized why she continues to be the most popular member of the royal family. The Queen has a great sense of humor, unlike her much less popular son and daughter-in-law. (Relieve tension in the atmosphere by some appropriate action or remark.)

10. My language teacher always uses THE QUEEN'S ENGLISH. (Standard English in the UK. In Shakespeare's time "the Queen" would have been Elizabeth the First, not Elizabeth the Second, who is now reigning. I suppose that when Prince Charles becomes King, we'll speak of "the King's English." Of course, nowadays all kinds of English are used, even on the UK's BBC. They are all acceptable as long as they can be clearly understood.)

11. During the typhoon last night, I DIDN'T SLEEP A WINK*. (I got absolutely NO sleep.)

12. I thought I had bought a valuable Ming Dynasty vase in Beijing last year, but it turned out to be a fake worth nothing. Sadly I realized that ALL THAT GLITTERS IS NOT GOLD*. (Something that looks like gold or seems very valuable may actually be worthless.)

13. My grandson tried to show me how his computer works, but frankly, everything he said WAS GREEK TO ME*. (Be hard to understand, like the difficult Greek language. It is possible that I had to retire early from my company because I couldn't deal with computers well.)

14. Before they started paying taxes, the family had lived extravagantly, but now in their small rented house, they looked quite poor. There was no doubt that THEY HAD SEEN BETTER DAYS*. (People or things that were once new or rich-looking now seem shabby and poor.)

15. I've warned my daughter about the handsome drug addict that she hopes to marry, but she won't face the truth. Yes, LOVE IS BLIND*. (It's difficult to see the faults of a person you're in love with.)

16. Everyone was worried when a little boy disappeared in the forest, but in the end they found him sleeping happily in an army hut. As they say, ALL'S WELL THAT ENDS WELL*. (Even if a situation starts off badly, everything is fine if it ends on a happy note.)

17. I gave Mr. Morgan five million yen to invest for me, but now I can't find him ... or my money! They just seem to have VANISHED INTO THIN AIR*. (Disappear without leaving a trace.)

18. I dream of playing golf TO MY HEART'S CONTENT* after I retire. (Do something until you're completely satisfied.)

19. Although Mrs. Jones is 80, she insists on dressing like a young teenager. I suppose she thinks she looks cute, but actually she's made herself a LAUGHINGSTOCK*. (A person who seems ridiculous and is laughed at by others.)

20. It is alleged that body parts from the tigers at Tiger Temple in Thailand were being sold, so the government will close it down. It will be A GOOD RIDDANCE*. (Getting rid of something will be of great benefit — in this case,

a benefit to both people and animals.)

At first you may have thought Shakespeare's quotations to be difficult, but now you see how easy they are to understand and use. It just goes to prove, ALL'S WELL THAT ENDS WELL!

Notes

Notesで解説を加えた文・表現には＊を印してあります。
[　]は当該の文・表現が記載されたページおよび行数を示しています。

Two Amazing "Rags to Riches" Stories from Scotland

[*p.*8 タイトル] **Rags to Riches**：「無一文から大金持ちへ」。(from) rags to riches は成句で、go from rags to riches は「赤貧から大金持ちになる」。rag は「ぼろ布、ぼろ着」「布きれ」。red rag to a bull は文字どおりには「雄牛に赤布」で「怒りを挑発するもの」という意味の口語表現。riches は複数扱いの名詞で「財産」「富」「豊かさ」「(天然)資源」。Riches have wings.「金には羽がある」「お金はお足」、Riches do not always bring happiness.「富は必ずしも幸福をもたらさない」という表現がある。

[*p.*8 *l.*7] **multimillionaires**：millionaire「百万長者」の上を行くのが multimillionaire「億万長者、大富豪」。

[*p.*8 *l.*12] **Asperger syndrome**：「アスペルガー症候群」。発達障害のひとつで、対人コミュニケーションに困難があり、知的障害や言葉の発達の遅れはない。

[*p.*8 *l.*18] **persevered with**：persevere with ... は「(努力・仕事などを)頑張ってやり通す、刻苦勉励する」。

[*p.*9 *l.*4] **upset**：「動揺して」。形容詞の upset は「気持ちが乱れて、腹を立てて」など平静を失うこと。動詞の upset は「(物を)ひっくり返す」が中心的意味で「(計画などを)狂わせる」「(人を)動揺させる」「(組織を)転覆させる」など多くの意味を持つ。

[*p.*9 *l.*17] **return**：ここでの return はイギリス英語で「往復(の)」。アメリカ英語では round-trip。「片道切符」はイギリス英語では single ticket、アメリカ英語では one-way ticket。

[*p.*9 *l.*22] **the great day**：「運命を決したその日」。ここでの great は day と結び付いて「重大な、重要な」。

[*p.*10 *l.*4] **ventured on stage**：「思い切ってステージに上がった」。venture は「思い切ってやってみる」。

[*p.*10 *l.*7] **Why bother to listen?**：「別に聴かなくていいんじゃない?」。why bother to ... は「なぜ～しなければいけないのか、そんな必要はないだろう」。ここでの bother は「わざわざ～する」。

[*p.*10 *l.*13] **was thunderstruck**：「びっくり仰天した」。be thunderstruck「驚愕する」は文字どおりには「雷に打たれる」だが、この意味では使われない。「あの木に雷が落ちた」なら The lightning struck the tree. などとなる。

[*p.*10 *l.*16] **thunderous**：「とどろくような、雷鳴のような」

[*p.*11 *l.*10] **She projects an air of sincere, innocent simplicity**：「彼女からは誠実で純朴な人柄が感じられる」。ここでの project は「(イメージなどを)人に印象づける」。an air of ... は「(人の)～な様子・態度」。an air of confidence なら「自信に満ちた態度」。sincere は「誠実な、裏表のない」。innocent は「純真な」。simplicity は「素朴さ」。

[*p.*11 *l.*12] **plump**：「ふっくらした、ぽっちゃりした」。fat「太った」

131

の好意的な表現。

- [p.11 l.17] **had a meltdown**:「パニックを起こした」。meltdown は「炉心溶融」だが、「(機構などの)崩壊、(株価の)急落、(コンピューターの)機能停止」なども意味する。
- [p.12 l.12] **demons**:「苦しみの種」。demon は「悪魔、(〜の)鬼」だが、複数形で「(否定的な感情など)人を苦しめるもの」。
- [p.12 l.15] **clinical depression**:「臨床的鬱病」。抑鬱気分があり、物事に対する興味や関心が低下する心の症状や、体重の減少、疲れやすい、不眠といった体の症状が現れる。
- [p.12 l.16] **contemplating suicide**:「自殺を考えていた」。contemplate は「(〜することを)考える」。suicide は「自殺」。
- [p.12 l.17] **on welfare**:「生活保護を受けて」。welfare は「福祉」「生活保護手当」。
- [p.12 l.23] **lodgings**:「下宿」。この意味では一部屋でも lodgings と複数形で使われる。
- [p.13 l.5] **Quite possibly**:「おそらくは」。quite は「まったく」。possibly は「ことによると、もしかすると」で、これから述べる意外なことなどを強調する。
- [p.13 l.8] **bespectacled**:「めがねをかけた」。spectacles は glasses「めがね」の古風な言い方。「接頭辞 be- +身に着けるもの+語尾 -ed」で形容詞をつくり、「〜で覆われた、〜をまとった」を表す。bejeweled「宝石で飾った」はゲーム名にもなっている。
- [p.13 l.15] **rejection slips**:「断り状、不採用通知」。rejection は「拒絶、却下」。slip は「細長い紙、メモ、付箋」。
- [p.13 l.19] **was thrilled to bits**:「ものすごくうれしかった」。to bits「とても」はイギリス英語で be thrilled や love などとよく使われる。
- [p.13 l.21] **on the verge of ...**:「〜する寸前で」
- [p.14 l.5] **measly**:「ほんのわずかの、たった〜ぽっちの」
- [p.14 l.5] **advance**:「アドバンス、印税前払い金」
- [p.14 l.16] **millions, if not billions**:「何十億とは言わないまでも何百万かは」。A if not B は「B とは言わないまでも A (以上)は」。
- [p.14 l.22] **silver lining**:「光明」。Every cloud has a silver lining.「どんな雲にも(太陽が当たって)銀色に輝く縁取りがある」「どんな不幸にも何かしら希望が見いだせる」ということわざから。最後の文はこのことわざを下敷きにしている。

Unmade Bed Sells for $4,000,000!

- [p.15 l.3] **True to its name**:「その名前どおり」。true to ... は「〜と一致した」「〜と寸分違わない」という意味。a portrait true to life で「実物そっくりの肖像画」、true to the original は「原物にそっくりの」「原文に忠実な」という意味になる。
- [p.15 l.3] ***My Bed***:「マイ・ベッド」。イギリスを代表する若手アーティスト、トレーシー・エミン(1963 〜)の前衛的な芸術作品。自分が

4日間過ごしたあとの乱れたベッドをそのまま展示し、美術界に衝撃を与えた。エミンは私的で性的な記憶にまつわる作品を多く制作することで知られ、動物のホルマリン漬け作品で有名なダミアン・ハースト (1965～) などとともに、"Young British Artists" (YBA) のひとりとして、衝撃的な作品の創作を続けている。

[p.15 l.4] **dirty unmade bed**:「汚れたぐちゃぐちゃのベッド」。unmade は「(ベッドが) 整えられていない」という形容詞。make a / the bed で「ベッドを整える」、bedmaking は「ベッドメイキング、ベッドを整えること」。

[p.15 l.5] **shortlisted**:「最終選考に残った」「最終候補者名簿に入った」。short list は名詞で「最終選抜候補者名簿 / リスト」のこと。動詞の shortlist は、主に受身で、「最終候補者名簿に掲載される」という意味になる。

[p.15 l.6] **Turner Prize**:「ターナー賞」。19世紀イギリスのロマン主義の画家 J.M.W. Turner (1775～1851) にちなみ、イギリス人またはイギリス在住の美術家に与えられる賞。国立美術館テート・ブリテンが主催し、選考会・授賞式はテレビで生中継される。

[p.15 l.7] **did win its creator a lot of attention**:did は次にくる動詞の意味を強める助動詞の過去形、win a lot of attention は「大きな注目を浴びる」、creator は「制作者」「作者」のことで、「その作者が大きな注目を浴びた / 獲得した」となる。「win +人 ...」で「人に～を得させる」という意味になる。

[p.15 l.18] **Christie's**:「クリスティーズ」。Sotheby's (サザビーズ) と並ぶ世界的に有名なオークションハウス。著名な芸術作品のみならず、ダイアナ妃やマリリン・モンロー、ナポレオンなど歴史上の人物に関連した美術品,個人財産なども競売にかけられる。芸術・装飾分野の教育機関も有し、卒業生の多くが競売会社の職員や美術商、美術評論家、美術館学芸員、美術書編集者など美術界の第一線で活躍する。

[p.16 l.2] **business acumen**:「ビジネス感覚」「商才」。acumen は「鋭い洞察力」「眼識」のこと。

[p.16 l.12] **wayward daughter's untidy bedroom**:「親の言うことを聞かない娘の散らかった寝室」。wayward は「言うことを聞かない」「わがままな」「従順でない」という形容詞。untidy は「散らかった」「だらしない」「ずさんな」。tidy「きちんとした」「整然とした」「きれい好きの」の前に、「反」「非」「不」を示す接頭辞の un- が付いた形容詞。

[p.16 l.16] **knickers**:ここではイギリス英語で「女性用パンティー」のこと。膝下までのゆったりした短ズボンも意味するが、これは knickerbockers とも呼ばれる。日本でも登山用の短いズボンのことを「ニッカーボッカー」と言うが、これはもともと「ニューヨークのオランダ移民やその子孫」のことで、彼らがはいていた短ズボンに由来する。

[p.16 l.17] **strewn about ...**:「～(の上) にまき散らされた」。strewn は、strew「まき散らす」「ばらまく」の過去分詞。

[*p.16 l.18*] **convincingly**：副詞で「説得力をもって」「もっともらしく」。動詞の convince は「確信させる」「納得させる」、形容詞の convincing は「説得力のある」「なるほどと思わせる」。

[*p.16 l.20*] **in that respect**：「その点において」「その点では」。「尊敬（する）」という意味の respect には、「点」「事項」「箇所」という意味もあり、in all respects で「すべての点において」、in some respects で「いくつかの点で」、in one respect で「ある点で、ある意味で」などの表現がある。

[*p.16 l.23*] **unapologetic**：「弁解しない」「非を認めない」。反対語は apologetic「申し訳なさそうな」で、その名詞は apology「謝罪」「わび」、動詞は apologize「謝る」。

[*p.17 l.1*] **the LAST artistic expression I would want**：「私が最後に望むであろう芸術的表現」とは「私が絶対に望ましいとは思わない芸術に関する表現」という意味。the last to do、あるいは「the last that ＋文」には、「最も～しそうもない」「とても～とは思えない」「最も好ましくない / 不適切な」という意味があり、例えば She would be the last person to betray you. は「彼女はあなたを裏切るような人ではない」、He is the last guy I'd want my daughter to marry. なら「彼には絶対に私の娘の夫になってほしくない」となる。

[*p.17 l.2*] **as the saying goes, "Beauty is in the eye of the beholder"**：「ことわざにあるように、『美は見る人の目の中にある』のだ」。behold は「見る」という意味の動詞で、それに -er がついて「見る人」となる。古代ギリシャ時代に生まれたこのことわざの意味は「何を美しく思うかは、人それぞれ違う」という意味。日本語なら、「蓼食う虫も好き好き」「あばたもえくぼ」となる。

[*p.17 l.8*] **perception**：「鑑識眼」「感覚」「見識」。形容詞は perceptive「知覚の」「知覚力のある」「知覚の鋭い」、動詞は perceive「知覚する」「理解する」。

[*p.17 l.9*] **gimmick**：「(人目を引くための) 巧妙な仕掛け」「(手品の) タネ」「トリック」。広告で注意を引くための「策略」「新機軸」「仕掛け」「新しい案」という意味でも使用される。

[*p.17 l.11*] **masquerade as works of art**：「芸術作品に変装する / なりすます」。masquerade は「仮面舞踏会」のことだが、ここでは動詞で「変装する」「仮装する」「なりすます」。

[*p.17 l.20*] **on behalf of**：「～の代わりに」「～の代理で」「～を代表して」

[*p.17 l.23*] **WHERE on earth would you put it?**：「それ (*My Bed* という作品) を一体どこに置くって言うんだ？」。on earth は疑問符とともに使用されるときには「一体全体」という強調の意味になる。「地上で」「この世で」「世界中で」という意味もあり、クリストファー・ロイド著の『137 億年の物語』(文藝春秋) という本があるが、その原題は "What on Earth Happened?"。これは on Earth が「一体全体」と「地球上で」の両方の意味に解釈でき、とてもしゃれていて魅力的なタイトルになっている。

[*p.18 l.3*] **thorny problem**：「やっかいな問題」。thorn は「トゲ」「イ

バラ」のこと。thorny は形容詞で、「困難な」「トゲだらけの」「イバラの」という意味。thorny path で「イバラの / 苦難の道」、thorny issue なら「頭の痛い問題」となる。

[p.18 l.5] **unkempt splendor**：unkempt はもともと「櫛でとかしていないので、髪の毛がボサボサの」という意味の形容詞。「がさつな」「散らかった」「洗練されていない」「あか抜けしない」という意味でも使われる。splendor は「華麗さ」「壮麗さ」「見事さ」のこと。*My Bed* のような「ぐちゃぐちゃ」に見える作品が、テートのような格調高く壮麗な美術館に展示されているというギャップをユーモラスに表現している。

[p.18 l.6] **raking in the millions**：rake in the millions は「熊手を使って百万単位で金をかき集める」ということで、「荒稼ぎする」「ぼろもうけする」という意味。rake はもともと「熊手」「熊手でかき集める」だが、「(他人の過去などを) 暴き出す」という意味もある。

[p.18 l.11] **fetched**：fetch は「取って / 持ってくる」「引き出す」「魅了する」などの意味があるが、ここでは「〜で売れる」ということ。fetch a good price なら「良い値で売れる」となる。

[p.18 l.12] **make *My Bed* a bargain**：bargain には「掘り出し物」「格安品」「特売品」「お買い得品」「セール」などの意味がある。「*My Bed* を格安品にする」とは、「ほかの作品が高い値で売れたので、とてつもなく高額に思えた *My Bed* でさえ安く感じる」ということ。

[p.19 l.1] **vulgar**：「卑猥な」「猥褻な」「下品な」。ほかにも「通俗的な」「これ見よがしの」などの意味がある。

[p.19 l.4] **eBay**：「イーベイ」。1995 年に米国で設立された世界最大のネットオークション・サイト。自宅に居ながらにして、世界中に散らばる売り手と買い手がネットを介して売買できるサービスで人気となっている。

[p.20 l.3] **inviting-looking**：「気をそそられるような外見 / 姿をした」。inviting は「誘惑するような」「魅力的な」、looking は「〜のような姿 / 顔つきの」という意味。よく「美しい」「かっこいい」という意味で good-looking という表現が使われ、例えば Hank Williams が歌った "Hey, Good Lookin'" という歌がある。ほかに -looking を使用した表現には、young-looking「若そうに見える」、angry-looking「怒ったような表情の」など。

[p.20 l.8] **tarantula spider**：「クモのタランチュラ」。語源はイタリアの都市「タラント」とされ、この地方の伝説に登場する毒グモ。このクモに刺されると、タランティズム (舞踏病) という病気になるが、タランテラという踊りを踊れば助かるという伝承があった。この地方には、実際に大型のクモが生息するが、かまれて死ぬほどの毒はない。ヨーロッパ人が新大陸に渡ったあと、恐ろしい姿の大型グモをタランチュラと呼ぶようになった。

[p.20 l.9] **black widow**：「クロゴケグモ」。widow は日本語で「未亡人」のことで、「クロゴケ」の漢字表記は「黒後家」となる。北アメリカ大陸に広く分布する黒いクモで、毒性が強い。

[p.20 l.15] **celebrated**：形容詞で「名高い」「有名な」。動詞の

celebrate は「祝う」「世に知らせる / 公表する」「賛美する」、名詞は celebration で「称賛、賛美」「祝典、祝賀会」となる。

Athletes Who Make All the Right Choices—and the Wrong Ones

[p.21 タイトル] **Athletes**:「運動選手」。athlete は多様なスポーツの選手や愛好家を指すが、もともとは「陸上競技の選手」を意味し、イギリス英語ではそちらのイメージが強い。

[p.21 l.3] **The world is your oyster.**: The world is A's oyster. は「何でも A の思いのまま」。シェークスピアの "The Merry Wives of Windsor"「ウィンザーの陽気な女房たち」の Why, then the world's mine oyster. Which I with sword will open.「世の中は俺の牡蠣。剣でこじ開けるまで。さすれば俺のものさ」から。力ずくで手に入れるニュアンスが抜け落ち、今では前途洋々な人などについて使われる。

[p.21 l.8] **NFL**: National Football League (NFL) は、米国のアメリカンフットボールのプロリーグ。

[p.21 l.9] **was in line to sign**:「サインすることになる」。be in line はもともと「(何かのために) 並ぶ」こと。そこから「〜が整っている、(地位など) を手に入れる可能性が高い、〜が起こりそうだ」。

[p.21 l.14] **luxurious million-dollar mansion**:「百万ドルの豪邸」。luxurious は「(ものが) 豪華な」。million-dollar は「百万ドルの」。ハイフンでつないで形容詞的に使われている。mansion は「大邸宅」。日本語の「マンション」の元になった語だが、集合住宅を表す英語は apartment や condominium (condo)、イギリス英語では flat。

[p.21 l.15] **fiancée**:「婚約者、フィアンセ (女性)」。「婚約者 (男性)」は fiancé。新聞などでは、fiancee、fiance とアクセント記号のない表記も見受けられる。

[p.21 l.16] **dearly**:「深く、心から」。dear の副詞形で、比較級、最上級は more dearly、most dearly になる。

[p.21 l.20] **Yet**:「しかし」。「まだ (〜でない)」という意味でおなじみの yet だが、ここでは、前述の内容と対照的なことを述べる前置きに使われている。

[p.22 l.3] **prison cell**:「刑務所の独房」。cell は「細胞」という意味もあるが、ここでは「独房」のこと。

[p.22 l.4] **He had committed suicide by hanging himself with a sheet.**:「彼はシーツで首をつって自殺していた」。遺体が発見される前のことなので had committed と過去完了形になっている。commit suicide は「自殺する」。suicide は「sui (自己) + cide (殺害)」で「自殺」。「殺人」なら「homicide (人＋殺害)」で、意図的・計画的な殺人 (murder) と計画性のない殺人 (manslaughter) の両方を含む。hang oneself は「首をつる」、hang A は「A を絞首刑にする」。

[p.22 l.5] **What had gone so badly wrong**:「それほどに身を誤るような何があったのか」。go wrong は「(物事が)うまくいかない、(人

が)道を間違える」。
- [p.22 l.7] **a young athlete of such promise**:「若くこんなに前途有望な運動選手」。ここでの promise は「将来の見込み」で、of promise は「(将来を)約束された、嘱望されている」。
- [p.22 l.13] **mix with young gang members**:「若いギャング連中とつるむ」。mix with A は「A と付き合う」。gang は「ギャング、不良グループ、暴力団」。gangster は「(ひとりの)ギャング」。
- [p.22 l.15] **barhopping**:「はしご酒、飲み歩き」。この hop は「あちこち渡り歩く」こと。「お寺巡り」なら temple hopping などと言えるだろう。
- [p.22 l.16] **descent into hell**:「地獄への転落」。descent は「下降、転落、堕落」。hell は「地獄」。
- [p.22 l.17] **the low point of his life**:「人生最悪の時」。low point は「最低・最悪の事態」。
- [p.22 l.19] **deserted**:「さびれた、人が住まない」
- [p.22 l.20] **after giving him a ride**:「彼を乗せてやったあとで」。give A a ride は「(車に)A を乗せる」。
- [p.22 l.22] **almost killed**:「もう少しで殺すところだった」。almost は動詞の前で「危うく(〜するところ)」。
- [p.22 l.24] **was permanently blinded in his right eye**:「永久に右目の光を失った」。permanently は「永久に」。be blinded は「視力を失う、目がくらむ」。
- [p.23 l.1] **this case was hushed up**:「この事件はもみ消された」。case は「事件、案件」。hush up ... は「(事件などを)もみ消す、(人を)口止めする」。
- [p.23 l.3] **If he had been, a life might have been saved.**:「彼が起訴されていれば、ひとりの命は救われたかもしれない」。been の後に prosecuted が略されている。
- [p.23 l.5] **the first-degree murder**:「第 1 級謀殺罪」。最も悪質な殺人に対する罪。
- [p.23 l.6] **was found guilty**:「有罪とされた」。find A ... は「(陪審・法廷が)A に〜の評決・判決を下す」。
- [p.23 l.7] **sentenced to life in prison without the possibility of parole**:「保釈の可能性なしの終身刑を宣告された」
- [p.23 l.9] **pin down**:「〜を正確に知る、(原因などを)突き止める」
- [p.23 l.10] **was high on drugs**:「ドラッグでハイだった」
- [p.23 l.11] **imagined he had been insulted**:「自分が侮辱されたと思い込んだ」。ここでの imagine は「(真実でないことを真実と)思い込む」。insult は「(人を)侮辱する」。
- [p.23 l.12] **touchy type of person**:「すぐにかっとなりやすいタイプの人」。touchy は「激しやすい」。type は「タイプ、類型」。different type of shogi chess player なら「ひと味違うタイプの将棋棋士」。
- [p.23 l.15] **While there's life, there's hope**:「命あっての物種」。文字どおりには「命があるうちは希望がある」。

[p.23 l.25] **get on the wrong side of the law**:「法を破る」

[p.24 l.4] **arrogant, overpaid sportsmen**:「傲慢で超高給取りのスポーツ選手たち」。arrogant は「傲慢な、横柄な」。overpaid は「(給料などを) もらいすぎの」。sportsman はもともと「趣味で狩猟・釣りをする人」。「スポーツマン」の意味では athlete のほうが一般的。

[p.24 l.6] **making a bad scene**:「ひどい大騒ぎをして」。make a scene は「大騒ぎする」。

[p.24 l.7] **footballer**:「サッカー選手」

[p.24 l.8] **to behave himself**:「行儀よくするように」。behave oneself は「行儀よくする」。

[p.24 l.11] **f--- off**:「うせやがれ」。きわめて汚い罵りの言葉 four-letter word「4文字語」が含まれているために伏せ字になっている。テレビならピー音で消されるところ。

[p.24 l.12] **rowdy**:「(行動などが) 乱暴な、けんか好きな」

[p.25 l.3] **uncommon**:「普通でない、非凡な、並外れた」

[p.25 l.4] **small build**:「小さな体」。この build は「体格」。

[p.25 l.5] **unconventional**:「従来とは異なる、型にとらわれない」

[p.25 l.6] **early on**:「早い時期から」

[p.25 l.13] **partying**:「パーティーに出かけること」「夜遊び」

[p.25 l.14] **limber**:「(体が) 柔軟な、機敏な」

[p.25 l.16] **the course of the game**:「試合の流れ」

[p.25 l.17] **admirers**:「大ファン、崇拝者」

[p.25 l.17] **muscular hunk**:「ムキムキの筋肉マン」。muscular は「筋骨たくましい」。hunk は「マッチョタイプの男性」。

[p.25 l.18] **to get on in baseball**:「野球で成功するために」。get on は「(仕事・分野で) 成功する」。

[p.26 l.3] **Albert Camus**: フランスの小説家アルベール・カミュ (1913-1960)。1957年にノーベル文学賞受賞。

[p.26 l.4] **Your life is the sum of all your choices.**:「人生とは自分が行った選択の総和である」

[p.26 l.11] **Handsome is as handsome does.**:「行いが立派な人が立派なのだ」「見目より心」。後の handsome は副詞で、全体を Handsome is that handsome does.、あるいは Handsome is he who does handsomely. とすると、わかりやすい。

The Amazing Story of Willy, the Cross-dressing Cuttlefish

[p.27 l.2] **mating behavior**:「交尾・交接行動」。名詞の mate「仲間」は、teammate「チームメート」、classmate「同級生」など、ほかの語と複合語をつくるほか、単独で「(つがいの) 一方」などの意味を持つ。A's mate とすれば「A (夫・妻) の連れ合い」、イギリス英語圏では「A の同性の友人」。ここでは動詞で「つがう、交尾・交接する」。behavior は「行動、ふるまい」。動詞は behave で、Behave yourself!「お行儀よくしなさい!」は親が子供に言う定番フレーズ。behave oneself は「自制心をもって行動する」こと。

- [*p.27 l.3*] **cuttlefish**：cuttlefish はモンゴウイカなど体(外套膜)が短く石灰質の甲を持つ「コウイカ」類を指す語。一方、細長い体で薄い軟甲を持つ「ヤリイカ、スルメイカ」類は squid と言う。
- [*p.27 l.4*] **cross-dressing, or transvestite**：cross-dressing は「cross-(交差する、横断する)＋dress(服を着る)」という動詞を元にした名詞で「異性の服を着ること」。transvestite は trans-(ほかの側へ)＋*vestire*(ラテン語の「服を着せる」)からきた形容詞・名詞で、「服装倒錯(の)、異性の服を着る(人)、女装する(人)」。ここでは同様の意味の語を or で言い換えて、「メスに擬態する」(mimic female) ことを示している。
- [*p.27 l.6*] **texture**：「質感」。texture は接触して風合いを感じることで、「手ざわり、感触」「(織物の)織り具合、生地」「(食べ物の)食感」「(芸術作品の)質感」などを意味する。
- [*p.27 l.9*] **surmise**：「推測する、臆測する」
- [*p.27 l.11*] **work out**：work out は「(金額や数字が)～になる」「(物事が)うまくいく」「体を鍛える」など多くの意味を持つが、ここでは「(問題を)解決する」。
- [*p.27 l.15*] **In the blink of an eye**：「一瞬のうちに」という意味の成句。blink は「まばたき」、動詞では「まばたきする、(光などが)点滅する、星がまたたく」。
- [*p.27 l.19*] **read up on**：read up on / about ... は「～についてたくさん読んで学ぶ、読みあさる」。
- [*p.28 l.3*] **through cunning and daring**：「巧みかつ大胆な方法で」。この through は「～の手段によって」。cunning は「ずる賢さ、巧妙さ」。日本語の「カンニング」の元になった語だが、それは cheating on an exam などと言う。daring は「大胆さ」。
- [*p.28 l.9*] **tentacles**：「触手、(イカの特に長い2本の)触腕」。tentacles は複数形で、「(外部からの)影響力、魔の手」という意味で使われることもある。
- [*p.28 l.11*] **didn't dare get too close**：「近寄ろうともしなかった」。dare (to) do ... は「あえて～する、思い切って～する」。dare は前出の daring の動詞形。get too close は文字どおりには「近づきすぎる」。
- [*p.28 l.14*] **bullying poses**：bullying は「いじめ」、pose は「ポーズ、態度」。ここでは「威嚇行動」をユーモラスに表現したもの。bully は動詞で「いじめる」、名詞で「いじめっ子」。
- [*p.28 l.18*] **might die a virgin**：「童貞のまま死ぬかもしれない」。virgin は「異性との性交渉の経験がない人」で男性も女性も指す。また、大文字の the Virgin は「聖母マリア」。
- [*p.28 l.20*] **get through**：「(隙間などを)なんとか通り抜ける」
- [*p.28 l.22*] **the beauty he wanted so badly to know**：「彼がなんとしてもお近づきになりたい美女」。beauty は「美女」。"Beauty and the Beast" はディズニー映画「美女と野獣」の原題。so badly は「どうしても(ほしい)」。know A は場合によって「A と知り合いである、A と懇意である、A と性的関係がある」などと意味

に幅がある。

- [p.29 l.3] **cross gender lines**:「性別を超える」。cross は「超える、越える」、gender は「(社会的) 性、ジェンダー」「(生物学的) 性」、line は「線、境界線」。
- [p.29 l.7] **dull brown**:「くすんだ茶色」。dull は「(人や物事が) 退屈な」「(人や動作に) 活力が見えない」などの意味があるが、ここでは「(色が) くすんだ」。bright「鮮やかな」の反対語。brown は「茶色」。
- [p.29 l.10] **competition**:「ライバル」。「競争相手」というと competitor だが、competition には「競争」以外に「競争相手」という意味もある。
- [p.29 l.11] **of your choice**: ... of A's choice は「A の好みの〜、A が選んだ〜」。
- [p.29 l.13] **for all intents and purposes**:「(真実かどうかは別にして) 実際上」「ほぼ〜と言っていい」という意味のフレーズ。intents も purposes も「目的、趣旨」という意味。
- [p.29 l.18] **sought a bit of romance**:「ちょっかいを出した、言い寄った」。sought は seek「〜を手に入れようとする」の過去形、a bit of は「ちょっとした〜」、romance は「恋愛関係、情事」。
- [p.29 l.19] **After some close calls**:「何度か危ない目に遭いながら」。close call は「危機一髪、(野球などの) きわどい判定」。
- [p.29 l.20] **in the presence of**: in the presence of A、または in A's presence は「(重要人物である) A の面前で」。
- [p.29 l.24] **Once he figured that out**:「彼はそう悟るや」。once は「〜するとたちまち」、figure out ... は「〜であることがわかる、理由などを理解する」。
- [p.30 l.2] **love at first sight**:「一目ぼれ」。at first sight は「一目で、一見したところ」。
- [p.30 l.4] **courting**: court は名詞では「宮廷、法廷、(テニスなどの) コート」などの意味があるが、ここでは動詞で「求愛する」。
- [p.30 l.5] **in the Seventh Heaven**:「幸せの絶頂で、有頂天になって」。the Seventh Heaven は「(ユダヤ教で神の国とされる) 第七天、最上天」「至福の状態」。
- [p.30 l.6] **gender-bending adventure turned out to be well worth the risk**:「性を超えた冒険は危険を冒すだけの価値のあるものになった」。gender-bending は「性別や性に関する既成概念を超える」こと。bend は「(身を) かがめる」「(ものを) 曲げる」「(事実を) 歪曲する」などの意味を持つ動詞。turn out to be は「結果的に〜になる」。worth ... は「〜の価値がある、〜に見合う値打ちがある」。
- [p.31 l.3] **there are ten times more males than females**:「オスはメスの 10 倍多くいる」。
- [p.31 l.15] **by letting off a cloud of thick black ink in its face**:「そいつの顔に一発墨の煙幕をお見舞いすることで」。let off は「発砲する」「(熱・気体などを) 発する」。cloud はほこりや湯気などの「雲のようなもの」。ink はイカやタコの「墨」。コウイカの学名 sepia から、

「イカ墨」やそれからつくられた暗褐色の絵の具が sepia と呼ばれた。今では sepia は「セピア色」を指すことが多い。

[p.31 *l*.19] **burrow**:「(動物などが) 穴を掘る、(人や動物が) 隠れる」。キツネなどの「巣穴」も burrow。

[p.31 *l*.23] **strikes while the iron is hot**:「鉄を熱いうちに打っているのだ」。元の表現はもちろんことわざ Strike while the iron is hot.「鉄は熱いうちに打て」。

She Turned Her Dead Husband into a Diamond!

[p.32 *l*.1] **died of liver and throat cancer**:「肝臓と喉のがんで亡くなった」。die of は「(病気や飢えなど) で死ぬ」。祖国や主義主張のために「命をなげうつ」と言うときには die for を使う。liver は「肝臓」「レバー」のこと。古代ギリシャでは、肝臓は人間の感情や意欲の根源と考えられていて、そこを流れる血液の量が多ければ多いほど勇気や気力が湧くとされた。故に lily-livered (ユリのように白い肝臓をした) は、肝臓を流れる血液の量が少なく白くなっているということで、「臆病な」という意味になる。cancer「がん」の語源は、ギリシャ語で「カニ」という意味の *karkínos*。ヒポクラテスががんで亡くなった人の遺体を解剖した際に、がんの血管などの組織が「カニ」のように見えたことに由来する。

[p.32 *l*.3] **devastated**:「打ちのめされた」。devastate は「大きく落胆させる」「(気持ちに) 打撃を与える」。そのほかに「荒廃させる」「徹底的に破壊する」という意味もある。

[p.32 *l*.5] **cremation**:「火葬」。動詞は cremate「火葬にする」。ちなみに「土葬」は burial または interment、「鳥葬」は sky burial、「水葬」は burial at sea となる。

[p.32 *l*.6] **ashes**:ここでは複数形で「遺灰」のこと。ash は通常「灰」や「燃え殻」を意味する。

[p.32 *l*.7] **urn**:ここでは「骨つぼ」。脚や台座のある「つぼ」や「かめ」のことを言う。

[p.32 *l*.8] **where his ashes were to be scattered**:「どこに遺灰がまかれるのか」。to be ... は「〜の予定である」「〜のはずである」ということを意味する。scatter は「〜をまく」。

[p.32 *l*.12] **come up**:ここでは「話題に出る」。ほかにも「(ある高さまで) 達する」「成長する」「(太陽や星が) 昇る」「(人が) 近づく」「(問題などが) 生じる」など、さまざまな意味がある。

[p.32 *l*.18] **Br.**:Britain「イギリス」、または British English「イギリス英語」の略。

[p.32 *l*.19] **Am.**:America「アメリカ」、あるいは American English「アメリカ英語」の略。

[p.32 *l*.20] **coffin**:「(遺体を入れる) 棺」「棺桶」。主に英国で使われる。drive a nail into one's coffin で、悩み事や不摂生などが「(人の) 寿命を縮める」という意味になる。

[p.32 *l*.20] **casket**:「棺」「棺桶」。主にアメリカで使われる coffin の

婉曲表現。もともとは宝石などを入れる「小箱」のこと。

[p.33 l.6] **interchangeable**:「お互いに交換できる」「置き換え可能な」。interchangeable part で「互換性のある部品」となる。interchange は動詞で「交換する」「互いにやり取りする」「交互に起こる」、名詞では「交換」「やり取り」のほかに、高速道路の「インターチェンジ」という意味もある。

[p.33 l.9] **condolences**:condolence は「お悔やみ」「哀悼の言葉」「弔辞」のこと。「お悔やみ申し上げます」に相当する英語には多くの表現がある。英語本文にある May I offer my condolences / sympathy? 以外にも、Please accept my sincere condolences. や My deepest condolences for your aunt's death. などがあるが、故人や遺族との関係、口頭か書面かによって表現の仕方は異なる。

[p.33 l.10] **the deceased**:「the ＋形容詞」の形の名詞で「故人」のこと。形容詞で「死亡した」「亡き～」という意味もあり、deceased wife「亡き妻」などと言う。特に死亡して間もない人のことを言う場合が多い。

[p.33 l.22] **dispose of**:「処理する」「処分する」「決着／始末をつける」「取り決める」という意味の句動詞。dispose を使ったことわざに、Man proposes, God disposes.「人は計画し、神が決裁する」がある。これは「人事を尽くして天命を待つ」という意味。

[p.33 l.25] **convert ... into ~**:「…を～に変える／変換する」。convert には、ほかの宗教に「改宗する／させる」、ほかの主義に「転向する／させる」という意味もある。convert は名詞では「改宗者」「転向者」となる。名詞形の conversion は「転換」「改変」「改造」「改定」「(外貨の) 両替」「換金」などの意味。

[p.34 l.1] **diamond**:「ダイヤモンド」。天然の鉱物の中で最も硬く、屈折率が大きく、美しい光沢を持つ最高の宝石。ギリシャ語の *adámās*(征服しえない、屈しない)、およびラテン語の *adamas*(何物にも侵されない硬い物)に由来する。「ひし形」も意味し、トランプでは「ダイヤ」、野球用語では「内野」から「野球場」全体も意味するようになった。ケビン・コスナー主演の野球映画 "For Love of the Game" に、主人公の野球選手が恋人から「あなたは私よりも diamond を愛しているのね」と言って別れを告げられるシーンがあった。この場合の diamond は「野球」の意味。

[p.34 l.5] **carbon content**:「炭素含有量／含有物」。carbon は「炭素」。content には「内容物」「中身」「容量」「容積」「体積」などの意味がある。

[p.34 l.8] **carat**:「カラット」、宝石の重さの単位で約 200mg。karat と表記されることもある。語源は、ギリシャ語の *kerátion*「イナゴマメの実」。この豆は地中海沿岸やエジプトの温暖で乾燥した地域で育ち、大きさも重さも均一のためダイヤモンドの重さを量るのに使われたとされる。

[p.34 l.11] **thrilled**:「興奮した」「ワクワクした」「感激した」。英語の thrill は、日本語とは異なり、恐怖や不安だけでなく感動や喜びや楽しさなどでワクワクし興奮する場合にも用いられる。

- [*p.*34 *l.*12] **canary yellow**:「カナリー・イエロー（カナリア色）」。少し緑がかった明るい黄色のこと。鳥の canary「カナリア」はアフリカ大陸の北西岸に近いスペイン領のカナリア島に由来する。この島に「犬」が多かったことから、ラテン語で「犬」を意味する *canis* から *Canaria Insula*（犬の島）となり、この島に生息する鳥も canary と呼ばれるようになった。
- [*p.*34 *l.*19] **dubious**:「いかがわしい」「怪しいと思う」「疑わしい」「うさんくさい」。「真意のはっきりしない」「あいまいな」という意味もある。
- [*p.*34 *l.*20] **came round**:come round は、ここでは「意見を変える」「同調する」。ほかにも「ぶらりと立ち寄る」「（季節などが）巡る」「回覧される」「意識を取り戻す」などの意味がある。
- [*p.*34 *l.*24] **plural**:言語学用語で「複数（形）」のこと。「単数形」は singular。形容詞では「複数の」「2 つ以上の」という意味になる。
- [*p.*34 *l.*25] **set in**:「（宝石などを）はめ込む」
- [*p.*35 *l.*6] **confronted**:confront は「（問題などに）直面する」。名詞の confrontation は「（問題などと）向き合うこと」「対立」「（思想の）論争」など。
- [*p.*36 *l.*2] **anything to do with**:「～に関するあらゆること」
- [*p.*36 *l.*5] **be swept under the carpet**:sweep under the carpet とは、「不都合なことを秘密にして隠す」という表現。直訳すると「カーペットの下にゴミを掃いて見えなくする」。アメリカでは carpet ではなく rug（じゅうたん）とすることが多い。
- [*p.*36 *l.*8] **attitude**:「態度」や「姿勢」という意味で使用されるが、ここでは「（物事への）意見 / 考え」。
- [*p.*36 *l.*11] **remains**:ここでは「遺体」「亡骸」。語源はラテン語の *remanēre*(あとに残る/ とどまる)。remain には、ほかにも名詞で「遺跡」「残骸」「残り物」、動詞で「とどまる」「残っている」「～のままである」などの意味がある。
- [*p.*36 *l.*12] **encased**:encase は「～をケース(箱)に入れる」。incase とも言う。「中へ」を意味する接頭辞の en- や in- が case に付いた語。
- [*p.*36 *l.*12] **paperweight**:紙を押さえる「文鎮」。
- [*p.*36 *l.*13] **embedded**:embed は「(何かを)はめ込む」「埋める」「植え込む」。心や記憶に「深くとどめる」という意味もある。
- [*p.*36 *l.*15] **self-exploding hot air balloon**:「自動的に破裂する熱気球」。self-exploding は「自爆する」「みずから爆発する」。self- という接頭辞は「自己（の）」「自動（の）」という意味で、self-confidence で「自信」、self-conscious で「自意識過剰な」「人目を気にする」などとなる。ちなみに「スクーバダイビング」の SCUBA は self-contained underwater breathing apparatus の acronym（頭字語）。
- [*p.*36 *l.*19] **onlooker**:「傍観者」「見物人」「観衆」のこと。句動詞の look on「見物する、傍観する」に由来する。

How Maliwan Transformed an "Opium Village"

[p.37 l.2] **dirt-poor**：「非常に貧しい」「赤貧の」。生活に必要なものも資力もなく、ひどく困窮している状態を表す。dirt は名詞で「泥」「汚れ」のことだが、ここでは「土しかない」といったニュアンス。ちなみに競馬の「土や砂の走路」という意味もある（「芝のコース」は turf）。形容詞は dirty「汚い」「ずるい」。

[p.37 l.9] **instead**：「その代わりに」「それよりも」「そうしないで」という意味の副詞。As she couldn't go, I went instead. は「彼女が行けなかったので、代わりに私が行った」。instead of ... は「～の代わりに」。of のあとには名詞、動名詞だけでなく形容詞、不定詞あるいは as 節などがくる場合もある。Things are getting worse instead of better. なら「事態はよくなるどころか悪くなっている」という意味になる。

[p.37 l.10] **opium poppies**：opium は「アヘン」のことで、opium poppy はアヘンの原料となるケシ科ケシ属の植物。単に poppy と言う場合は、園芸用に栽培される「ヒナゲシ（corn poppy）」のことになる。ちなみに英国と清国の間で起こった「阿片戦争」は the Opium Wars。

[p.37 l.15] **sorry state**：「気の毒な状況」。sorry は「すまないと思って」という形容詞で、I am sorry.「すみません、申し訳ありません」などと言うが、ほかに「惨めな」「哀れむべき」「情けない」「粗末な」「くだらない」という意味もある。state は「状況」「状態」を表す一般的な単語。condition は「物事が成り立つ条件としての状態」、situation は「人や物との相互関係を重視した状況」、status は「公的・法的要因に基づく状態」という違いがある。

[p.38 l.9] **outlets**：outlet は「出口」「放出口」という意味だが、ここでは「販売代理店」「販売店」「販路」のこと。ほかにも工場直結の小売店「アウトレット」や「表現手段」「(作品の) 発表の場」「(感情の) はけ口」といった意味がある。また、主にアメリカでは電源コードの差し込み口「コンセント」も outlet と言い（イギリスでは socket）、consent と言っても通じない。差し込むほうは plug と言う。

[p.38 l.13] **once impoverished**：「かつて貧困にあえいでいた」。once は「昔」「ある時は」「かつては」、impoverished は形容詞で「貧しい」「貧弱な」という意味だが、土地が「不毛の」「やせた」というニュアンスがある。impoverish は「貧しくする」「(気力を) 衰えさせる」という動詞。

[p.38 l.13] **has been transformed into ...**：「～に一変していた」。transform は「変える」、change よりも硬く格調が高い語。transform into ... は「～に変える」。名詞は transformation「変化」。

[p.38 l.23] **ram**：「去勢されていない雄羊」。「去勢した雄羊」は wether と言い、weather「天気」や whether「～かどうか」と同じ発音。一般的に「羊」は sheep と言うが、「(成長した) 雌羊」は ewe、「子羊」は lamb。「羊の肉」は mutton、特に「(生後 12 か月以内の) 子羊の肉、ラム肉」は lamb と言う。ちなみに天文学や星占いの星座「牡羊座」

は Aries、あるいは the Ram。

[p.38 l.24] **ewes**:「(成長した)雌羊」。「雌の子羊」は ewe lamb となる。

[p.38 l.24] **arabica coffee**:エチオピア原産の「アラビカ種」と呼ばれる豆で淹れたコーヒー。世界で最も多く飲まれている。

[p.38 l.25] **looked after**: look after ... は「〜の世話をする」。look after a baby で「赤ん坊の世話をする」。ほかに「気を配る」「注意を払う」「監督する」といった意味もあり、Let the future look after itself. は「明日は明日の風が吹く」ということわざ。

[p.39 l.1] **put ... to full use**:「〜を十分に活用する、フルに活用する」。full の代わりに good を使って put ... to good use とすると「〜を有効活用する」、practical にして put ... to practical use は「〜を実用化する」となる。

[p.39 l.5] **deforested**: deforest は「森林を切り払う、切り開く」。forest は名詞で「森林」「山林」だが、動詞では「植林する」「(木を植えて)森林に変える」という意味になる。それに「反〜化する」という意味の接頭辞の de- を付けたもので、名詞の deforestation は「森林破壊」や「森林伐採」。

[p.39 l.9] **divine command**:「神の命令」。divine は「神聖な」「神の」「天与の」、command は「(権威を伴う)命令、指令」のことで、軍事用語では「司令部」「指揮権」を意味する。ちなみに divine judgment は「神の裁き」。

[p.39 l.11] **gave up growing**:「育てるのを諦めた」。give up は「諦める」「やめる」「放棄する」という意味の句動詞で、そのあとには give up smoking「禁煙する」のように動名詞や、give up alcohol「アルコールを断つ、禁酒する」、give up one's seat「席を譲る」のように名詞がくる場合もある。give up the ghost (霊を諦める) という表現は「人が死ぬ」という意味。

[p.39 l.11] **engaging in**: engage in ... は「〜に従事する」「〜に携わる」。engage in foreign trade は「外国貿易に携わる」。engage には「婚約させる」「約束する」という意味もあり、She is engaged to him. で「彼女は彼と婚約している」となる。「婚約指輪、エンゲージリング」は engagement ring。

[p.39 l.13] **seedlings**:移植用の「苗木」「若木」のこと。seed「種(をまく)」に -ling という「関わりあるもの」「小さく愛おしい」を意味する接尾辞が付いたもの。例えば、darling は「愛しの人」、duckling は「アヒルの子」、princeling は「幼少の王子」を意味する。

[p.39 l.13] **thrived**: この thrive は、植物が「成長する、繁殖する」。国や社会が「繁栄する」、人や事業が「成功する」という意味もある。形容詞は thriving で、thriving industry は「景気のいい産業」のこと。

[p.39 l.16] **reared**: ここでの rear は「(動物を)飼育する」。ほかに子供を「育てる」、植物を「栽培する」という意味もある。「育てる」には、ほかに bring up「人を育てる」、raise、breed「人や動物を育てる」、grow「植物を育てる」、nurse、foster「子供を育てる、世話をする」、train「訓練する、仕込む」、educate「教育する」などがある。rear には、ほかに「後ろ」という意味もあり、自動車の「バッ

クミラー」を rearview mirror と言う。

[p.39 l.17] **tackled**：tackle は「取り組む」「立ち向かう」「対処する」。名詞では「道具」という意味もあり、fishing tackle は「釣りの道具」。またラグビーやアメリカンフットボールの「タックル」ももちろん tackle。

[p.39 l.19] **yarn**：「（織物用の）糸」。spin cotton into yarn は「綿を紡いで糸にする」。口語では「つくり話」「冒険談」という意味もあり、spin a yarn で「冒険談／みやげ話をする」。

[p.39 l.19] **dyeing**：dye は「染める」「着色する」。名詞では「染料」となる。die「死ぬ」と発音が同じなので注意が必要。つづりは -ing がつく場合、「染める」が dyeing なのに対して、「死ぬ」は dying となる。

[p.39 l.20] **ground coffee**：「挽いたコーヒー」。ground は grind「すりつぶす」「すり砕く」「研ぐ」の過去形・過去分詞で、形容詞では「挽いて粉にした」という意味になる。つづりも発音も同じ ground「地面」と混同しないように注意が必要。

[p.39 l.21] **turmeric**：「ウコン」。ショウガ科の植物で、布や糸を黄色く染める染料となり、またスパイスとしてカレーなどにも使用される。

[p.39 l.21] **indigo**：「インディゴ」。マメ科の植物で、藍色に染める染料となる。indigo blue は「藍色」、indigo dyeing で「藍染め」となる。

[p.39 l.21] **placenta**：「胎盤」。語源はギリシャ語の *plakóenta*（平らなケーキ）。

[p.39 l.23] **byproducts**：「副産物」。「副次的な」を意味する接頭辞の by- と product「生産物」が結合した単語。ちなみに、薬などの「副作用」は side effect と言う。

[p.40 l.8] **was so appreciated**：「とても味わい楽しまれていた」。appreciate は「正しく評価する」「感謝する」という意味だが、「～の良さを味わう」「味わい鑑賞する」という意味でも使われる。また「物価が上がる、急騰する」という意味もあり、The price of land has appreciated greatly. で「地価がだいぶ上がった」となる。

[p.40 l.10] **Starbucks**：「スターバックス」。米国ワシントン州シアトル市に本社を持つコーヒーチェーン店。1971年の開業以来、全世界で数多くの店舗を展開している。

[p.40 l.12] **woolen**：「羊毛の」「ウールの」。wool「羊毛、ウール」の形容詞。woolen は名詞では「紡毛織物」「毛織物」「毛織の服」という意味になる。

[p.40 l.13] **shawls**：shawl は、女性用の「ショール、肩掛け」。動詞では「～にショールを掛ける」という意味。

[p.40 l.17] **itchy to the skin**：「肌がチクチクする、かゆい」。itchy は「かゆい」「ムズムズする」という形容詞だが、「したくてたまらない」「欲しくてムズムズする」「待ちかねてイライラする」という意味もあり、get itchy feet は「出かけたくてウズウズする」。

[p.40 l.22] **as long as a useful product is of the highest quality**：「役に立つ製品が最高の品質を備えているかぎりは」。as long as「～のかぎりは」「～であるならば」で、As long as you keep on trying, I'll help you. は「あなたが努力するかぎり、私はあなたを助けます」となる。is of the highest quality は「最高級の品質である」という意味だが、「be of 抽象名詞」で、その名詞が持つ抽象的特徴を表すことができ、形容詞で書き換えることもできる。例えば This book is of great importance.「この本は非常に重要だ」は This book is very important. と同じ意味になる。

[p.40 l.23] **is bound to sell**:「売れるはずだ」。bound は bind「縛る」の過去形・過去分詞だが、be bound to で「〜するはずである、運命にある」「〜する義務がある、しなければいけない」という意味になる。

[p.41 l.4] **country folk**:「田舎の人々」。folks と複数形で使うことも多い。town folk「都会の人々」、kinfolk「親族・同族」など特定の境遇の「人々」を表す。また、「国民」「民族」という意味でも使われる。形容詞では「庶民の」「民衆の」という意味があり、folk music は「民族音楽」、folk dance は「フォークダンス」。

[p.41 l.9] **civet**:アジア南部とアフリカに生息する「ジャコウネコ」。その下腹部から出る分泌液は「麝香」と呼ばれ、香水の原料となる。

[p.41 l.18] **come in contact with amino acids**:「アミノ酸と触れる」。come in contact with ... は「〜と接触する」。amino acid は「アミノ酸」。

[p.41 l.19] **digestive fluids**:「消化液」のことで、digestive juice とも言う。digest は「消化する」という意味で、名詞は digestion「消化」となる。digest には、ほかに「要約する」という意味もあり、この場合の名詞の「要約」は動詞と同じ digest となるが、アクセントが前にくる。fluid は「流動体」。形容詞では「流動的な」「変わりやすい」となり、fluid assets は「流動資産」。

[p.41 l.21] **excreted whole**:「丸ごと排泄された」。excrete は「排泄/排出する」。whole は名詞で「全体、全部、全員」、形容詞で「すべての」「完全な」「全体の」という意味だが、ここでは副詞で「丸ごと全部」、つまり「形を変えずに全部そのままで」という意味。

[p.41 l.21] **feces**:「糞」「大便」「排泄物」。イギリス英語では faeces とつづることもある。

[p.42 l.5] **bushes**:日本語で「ブッシュ」と言うと、草や笹などの生い茂った「やぶ」を思い浮かべるが、英語では、tree「木」より背の低い「低木」「灌木」を意味する。ほかには「田舎」「地方」「奥地」「未開地」など。

[p.42 l.6] **forbade**:forbid「禁じる、許さない」の過去形。「〜することを禁じる」は forbid のあとに ...-ing だけでなく that 節を置くこともできる。この場合、例えば School rules forbid that students use cell phones in class.「学校の規則では、生徒は教室で携帯電話を使うことが禁じられている」のように、that 節には否定の not が入らないことに注意。また forbid to do は「〜してはいけないと命じる」という意味になる。

[p.42 l.11] **intact**:「完全なまま」。ここではジャコウネコが排泄したコーヒー豆が「消化されずそのまま完全な形だった」ということを表現している。語源はラテン語の *intāctus*（触れられていない、手つか

ずの)。

[p.43 l.5] **goes for ...**:ここの go for は「~の値段で売れる、売られている」。例えば、My old car went for $3,000. で「私の古い車は3,000ドルで売れた」となる。

[p.43 l.14] **smoother drink**:「より口あたりのよい飲み物」。smooth は「滑らかな」「静かな」という意味だが、ここではコーヒーのことなので「口当たりのよい」。

[p.43 l.14] **go for it**:「それを好んでいる」。go for には「好む」「気に入る」「魅かれる」という意味もある。ちなみに go for it は「困難を承知で一か八かやってみる」という意味で、Go for it! は「がんばれ!」。

[p.43 l.20] **vintage**:「年代物の / 極上のワイン」。形容詞では、「優良な」「上等の」「銘柄の」などと良い意味で使われることが多いが、「古くさい」「時代遅れの」というネガティブな意味もある。

UK's Dangerous Craze For Meerkats as Pets

[p.45 タイトル] **Craze**:「大流行」「夢中」「(一時的な) 熱狂」のこと。He has a craze for jazz. で「彼はジャズに夢中である」といった表現になる。

[p.45 タイトル] **Meerkats**:「ミーアキャット」。アフリカ大陸南部の砂漠やサバンナの地中に巣穴を掘って生活する。「キャット」なのでネコ科と思われがちだが、meer のあとは cat ではなく kat で、マングース科の肉食動物。ペアもしくは家族単位、または複数のグループが集まって暮らす。前足を上げ、後足と尾を使って立ち、キョロキョロと周辺を見回す仕草で知られている。これは昼夜の寒暖差の激しい地域に生息するので、日中は巣穴から出て長時間日光浴をするためである。蛇や猛禽類といった外敵から身を守るために見張り役を立てて行動し、仲間同士は鳴き声で合図を交わす。

[p.45 l.3] **Aleksandr Orlov**:「アレクサンドル・オルロフ」。保険会社のウェブサイト等の広告に登場するミーアキャットのキャラクターで、ロシア貴族という設定になっている。アレクサンドルと彼の家族や友人たちが活躍するこのウェブ広告によって、会社は売り上げを倍増させた。Facebook で全世界に数多くのファンを持つ人気者となり、関連書籍や玩具なども多数販売されている。

[p.45 l.4] **demand**:「需要」。そのほかにも「要求」「必要負担」などの意味がある。on demand は「要求に応じて」という意味。IT用語ではインターネットやケーブルテレビを通じて、視聴者が見たい番組を見たいときに見ることのできるサービスのことを「オンデマンド」と言う。このほかに in demand「需要のある」、supply and demand「需要と供給」(日英で語順が逆) という表現がある。

[p.45 l.8] **potential owners**:「潜在的な飼い主」。ここでは「ミーアキャットを (今は飼っていないが)、将来飼いたいと思っている人」のこと。

[p.45 l.10] **In time**:ここでは「やがては」という意味。just in time (ちょうど間に合って) のように「時間内に」という表現もある。

148

[*p*.45 *l*.11] **give someone a nasty bite**：「誰かにひどくかみつく」。nasty は「ひどい」「危険な」という意味。nasty には、後半に出てくる nasty stain「落ちにくい汚れ、不潔なしみ」、nastier smell「もっと不愉快な / むかつくような臭い」のほかにも、「みだらな」「意地の悪い」「不機嫌な」や、あるいは「(天気が) 荒れ模様の」といった意味がある。

[*p*.45 *l*.11] **passing along**：pass along は通常「手渡す」「与える」「広める」「伝達する」だが、ここでは「感染させる」という意味。

[*p*.45 *l*.12] **bacteria**：「バクテリア」は「真正細菌」「細菌」。語源は「小さな杖」を意味するギリシャ語で、顕微鏡で観察した際に、微生物が「細い棒状」であったことに由来する。

[*p*.45 *l*.15] **roam**：「あてもなく歩き回る」「放浪する」「ぶらつく」。「心が落ち着かなかったり、好奇心にかられて広く歩き回る」という意味が強い。ちなみに、携帯電話やインターネット接続サービスで、契約しているサービス事業者のエリア外であっても、別の事業者を通じて同様のサービスを利用することを roaming「ローミング」と言う。

[*p*.45 *l*.16] **natural habitat**：「自然生息地」。habitat は「(動植物の) 生息地 / 生息環境」のほかに「(人の) 住居地」という意味もある。語源はラテン語の *habitat*（住んでいる）。

[*p*.45 *l*.18] **imply**：「暗示する」「ほのめかす」「意味する」。類義語に suggest、involve、hint などがある。名詞は implication「含蓄」「言外の意味」。

[*p*.46 *l*.4] **zoology**：「動物学」。zoo- は「動物の」、-logy は「学問」「〜論」「〜学」という意味。ちなみに zoo「動物園」は、zoological garden の短縮形。口語で a zoo とすると、「ひどく混雑 / 混乱している場所」「混乱状態」の意味になる。

[*p*.46 *l*.10] **cuddle up to Kimmy under her duvet**：「掛けぶとんの下でキミーに寄り添う」。duvet は「厚手の羽ぶとん」のこと。

[*p*.46 *l*.12] **stroked**：stroke は、ここでは「(手で) なでる」。ほかにも動詞で「オールを漕ぐ」「一撃を与える」、名詞の stroke には「脳卒中」の意味もある。

[*p*.46 *l*.13] **hyperactive**：「異常に活発な」。hyper- は「上」「超越」という接頭辞。類義語に super や ultra があり、厳密な意味を持つ分野ではスーパーを「超」、ハイパーを「極超」と訳す。hyperinflation「ハイパーインフレーション」とは、物価が短期のうちに数倍、数十倍に上がり、貨幣の社会的信頼が崩壊する経済状態のことを指す。

[*p*.46 *l*.15] **rubbing up against**：rub up against は「(〜に) 体をこすりつける」。

[*p*.46 *l*.19] **naughty**：「腕白な」「きかん気の」「手に負えない」。naughty boy で「腕白坊主」となる。ほかに「卑猥な / みだらな」という意味もある。

[*p*.46 *l*.24] **Crufts Dog Show**：ギネスブックでも認定された世界最大の「クラフツ・ドッグショー」。毎年3月に英国バーミンガムの国立エキシビションセンターで開催される。犬の品種ごとに、しつけ

や運動能力、美しさを競う種目が4日間にわたって繰り広げられる。

[p.47 l.1] **with whom they seem to identify**：関係代名詞 whom の前に with があるが、identify with で「～を同一視する」「～に自分を重ね合わせる」「～に共感する」という意味で、ここでは「ミーアキャットのキャラクター Aleksandr Orlov を、自分たちと同じ仲間であると認識しているように思える」ということを表している。

[p.47 l.5] **upkeep**：通常は「維持（費）」「扶養（費）」のことだが、ここでは「動物の飼育費」。

[p.47 l.6] **diet**：ここでは「エサ」「食事」「食物」。日本語に定着している「ダイエット」は「食事療法」「節食」という意味。国会のことを the Diet と言うが、こちらは中世ラテン語の dieta（1日の仕事→集会にあてられた1日）が英語になったのに対し、「ダイエット」は古代ギリシャ語の díaita（医者が指示した生き方→食事摂取規則）を語源としている。

[p.48 l.2] **depending on the point of purchase**：「購入時期によって」。depend on は「～によって決まる」「～しだいである」、point of purchase は「購買時点」という意味で POP と頭文字で省略されることもある。

[p.48 l.5] **buying ... on impulse**：「～を衝動的に買うこと」。impulse buy というフレーズで「衝動買い」、impulse buyer で「衝動買いをする人」という意味になる。

[p.48 l.14] **present**：ここでは「（そこに）いて／存在して」という意味の形容詞。例えば点呼をとるとき日本では「はい」と返事をするが、英語ではふつう "Here." と言い、改まった場では "Present, sir / ma'am." と返事をする。ちなみに present には「今（の）」「現在（の）」と「プレゼント、贈り物」という意味もある。インド出身のアメリカの医学博士 Deepak Chopra の自己啓発書 "The Seven Spiritual Laws of Success"（邦訳『富と成功をもたらす7つの法則』大和出版）には "The past is history, the future is a mystery, and this moment is a gift. That is why this moment is called 'the present.'"「過去は歴史であり、未来はミステリーだ。そしてこの瞬間は（神様からの）贈り物。だから、この瞬間は『present』と呼ばれる」という一節がある。英語における present の2つの意味を巧みに使用した名文である。

[p.48 l.19] **sentry**：「見張り番」、軍隊用語では「歩哨」。

[p.48 l.20] **run off to hide**：「隠れるために逃げ出す」。run off は「（人や動物などが）逃げる」のほかに、「（水などが）流出する」「～を印刷する（コピーする）」などの意味もある。

[p.48 l.24] **on the lookout for**：「～に目を光らせて」「～を警戒して」

[p.48 l.25] **predators**：predator は、ほかの生物を捕って食べることによって生存する「捕食動物」、「天敵」「略奪者」、さらには比喩表現で「（弱みにつけこんで）他人を利用する人」の意味で使用されることもある。1987年に、アーノルド・シュワルツェネッガー主演で同名の SF アクション映画が制作された。

Was the Nanny an Angel or a Devil?

[p.50 タイトル] **Nanny**:「乳母」「子守り」。幼児語で「おばあちゃん」という意味もある。動詞では「子守 / 乳母をする」「甘やかす」。国民の生活をあたかも乳母のように手厚く保護する「福祉国家」のことを、皮肉を込めて nanny state と呼ぶことがある。

[p.50 l.2] **fired**：fire は、ここでは「解雇する」。fire は「火」「火事」「(銃を) 発射する」だが、従業員を社会に向けて「発射する」、つまり「放逐する」ということから、「解雇する」という意味になった。

[p.50 l.3] **let alone ...**：否定文とともに用いて「~は言うまでもなく」「~はもちろん」。

[p.50 l.10] **Craigslist**:「クレイグスリスト」。1995 年にアメリカのサンフランシスコで始められたコミュニティーサイト。求人情報、不動産情報、コンサートや野球などのチケット情報など、ローカル情報を交換するために開設されたが、今では全世界の情報を掲載している。

[p.50 l.10] **outlet**：ここでは「発表の場」「表現の手段」。outlet は「出口」「(水や煙などの) 排出口」だが、商品が出ていく「販路」「小売店」という意味もある。日本にもある outlet mall (アウトレットモール) は、もともと「工場や倉庫から出てきた古いモデルや在庫過剰の商品を値下げして販売する直営店」のこと。また、電気器具のコードの差し込み口「コンセント」のことも outlet (イギリスでは socket) と言う。

[p.50 l.13] **found this out the hard way**：他人に教えてもらったのではなくて、「自分のつらい体験で学んだ」「経験から身にしみてわかった」。

[p.50 l.16] **references**：ここでの reference は「(推薦される人の) 身元保証人」「推薦者」。「参考文献」や「参照」という意味でも使われる。

[p.50 l.18] **You can't judge a book by its cover.**：「表紙で本の中身を判断することはできない」。「人やものは外見だけで判断することはできない」という意味のことわざ。日本語なら「人は見かけによらぬもの」。

[p.50 l.20] **fit into**：「適応する、順応する」。同じく「適応する」という意味の adapt to や adjust to に比べて、あまり努力せずに自然と「調和する」というニュアンスが強い。

[p.51 l.7] **sour**：形容詞で「すっぱい」という意味だが、ここでは動詞で「(関係などが) まずくなる / こじれる / 険悪になる」という意味。牛乳などが「すっぱくなる」から「腐敗する、腐る」、さらに「傷む」「悪くなる」というふうに意味が広がった。

[p.51 l.11] **sullen**:「ブスッとした」「無愛想な」。人以外にも「暗い」「陰鬱な」という意味で用いられ、sullen clouds は「どんよりした雲」、sullen sky「雲が低くたれこめた空」といった表現もある。

[p.51 l.17] **raid**：ここでは「(食べ物の容器や冷蔵庫などを) あさって食欲を満たす」という意味。raid は、もともと「急襲 (する)」「襲

撃(する)」だが、ほかに「(警察の) 手入れ」「押し込み強盗」「(株式買い付けの) 乗っ取り」という意味もあり、bank raid で「銀行強盗」、air raid で「空襲」、police raid は「警察の手入れ」などとなる。

[p.51 l.21] **ASAP**：as soon as possible「できるだけ早く」の略語。表現の頭文字を取った略語には、よく招待状などの最後に記される RSVP (Répondez, S'il Vous Plaît)「お返事ください」(フランス語)、パーティーの招待状に記す BYOB (Bring Your Own Booze / Beverage / Bottle)「酒類は各自ご持参ください」、TGIF (Thank God It's Friday)「ありがたい！ 今日は金曜だ」「花金」、FYI (For Your Information)「ご参考までに」などがある。最近ではメールで LOL (Laugh Out Loud)「爆笑」なども盛んに使われている。

[p.51 l.22] **had 'established residency'**：「居住権を確立した」。establish residency は「居住権を得る」「居住権の条件を満たす」という意味。

[p.52 l.6] **for heaven's sakes**：ここでは「いいかげんにしろ！」「冗談じゃない！」。ほかには、「どうかお願いだから」、「何てことだ！」、「一体全体何だって〜なんだ？」という意味でも使われる。

[p.52 l.8] **evicted**は「立ち退かせる」「強制退去させる」。建物や土地を不法に占拠している人を法律の手続きによって「追い出す」という意味。

[p.52 l.10] **complications**：「複雑な事態」「やっかいな問題」。形容詞は complicated「複雑な」。

[p.52 l.12] **board**：「食事」「賄い」のこと。bed and board で「宿泊と食事」という意味になる。「賄い付きの下宿」のことを boarding house と言う。

[p.52 l.14] **in the eyes of ...**：「〜の目に映るところでは」「〜の見地 / 観点から」。eye には「ものの見方」「見解」「観察の目」という意味がある。

[p.52 l.17] **initiate a lawsuit**：「裁判を起こす / 始める」。initiate には、ほかに「(正式な手続きを経て) 入会させる」「(正式の儀式によって) 奥義 / 秘訣を伝授する」「(条約や法律などを) 提案 / 発議する」、名詞で「新入会員」「秘伝 (を授けられた人)」という意味がある。名詞の initiation は「(正式の) 入会 (式)」「(秘法などの) 伝授 / イニシエーション」「創始、創業」。

[p.52 l.20] **put a padlock on ...**：「〜に南京錠を取り付けた」。padlock は「南京錠」のことで、「南京錠をかける」という動詞でも使われる。

[p.52 l.21] **gourmet food**：「グルメ向きの食べ物」。gourmet は「食通 (の)」「美食家 (の)」。もともとフランス語なので、最後の t は発音しない。「少年」「召し使い」から「ワイン商人の召し使い」「ワインに精通した人」という意味に変化し、そこから「食事の味に精通した人」「食通」となった。現代のフランス語にも、その名残として *gourmet* には「酒の鑑定士」という意味がある。

[p.52 l.22] **do the trick**：「うまくいく」「効き目がある」「功を奏する」「目的を達成する」。The third time does the trick. は「三度目の正直」。

[*p.*52 *l.*25] **key to the house**:「その家の鍵」。通常 key of the house ではなく to を使うことに注意。key には、日本語と同じように「(理解 / 解釈 / 達成するための) 手がかり」「秘訣」「手段」「謎」という意味もあり、例えば key to success で「成功の秘訣」、key to a bright future「輝かしい未来をつかむ手段」となる。

[*p.*53 *l.*6] **stands**:stand は「立つ」だが、ここでは「(ある状態の中に) ある / いる」という意味。

[*p.*53 *l.*7] **in the meantime**:「そうこうしているうちに」「その間に」。「ところで」「その一方で」という意味もある。

[*p.*54 *l.*2] **abused**:abuse ... は「(肉体的 / 精神的 / 性的に) 〜を虐待する」。「乱用する」という意味もある。名詞では「虐待」「悪弊」「罵り」という意味もあり、child abuse は「児童虐待」、alcohol abuse は「飲酒癖」、words of abuse は「暴言」となる。

[*p.*54 *l.*3] **verbally**:副詞で「言葉で」「言葉によって」という意味。形容詞は verbal「言葉の」「口頭の」で、verbal communication は「口頭伝達」つまり「言葉によるコミュニケーション」、verbal argument は「口げんか」、verbal protest は「言葉による抗議」。

[*p.*54 *l.*4] **frail**:「か弱い」「虚弱な」。物が「壊れやすい」「もろい」、主張などが「内容がない」「弱い」のほかに、健康・幸福・希望などが「はかない」という場合にも使われる。類似語には fragile や brittle がある。

[*p.*54 *l.*8] **SOMETHING for NOTHING**:「労せずに得る利益」「ただで何かを得ること」。ここでは「お金をまったく払わないのに、ナニーの労働を得ようとした」ということを意味している。この表現を使ったことわざに You don't get something for nothing.「ただでもらえるものは手に入らない」「ただより高いものはない」がある。

[*p.*54 *l.*10] **living out of a car**:live out of a car とは「車の中で寝たり食べたりして生活する」。live out of a cardboard box で「段ボール箱で生活する」となる。

[*p.*54 *l.*12] **exploit**:「搾取する」「利用する」「(人を) 食い物にする」。市場や資源などを「開拓する」「開発する」という意味もある。名詞で「偉業」「快挙」「英雄的行為」という意味もあり、the exploits of Alexander the Great は「アレクサンダー大王の偉業」。

[*p.*54 *l.*18] **titled**:title は名詞では「肩書」「題名」「称号」だが、ここでは動詞で「肩書を与える / 与えられている」から「(人) を〜と呼ぶ」という意味になる。

[*p.*54 *l.*18] **vexatious litigant**:「訴権乱用者」、つまり「嫌がらせで頻繁に訴訟を起こす人」のこと。vexatious は「いらだたしい」だが、法律用語として「訴権乱用の」という意味がある。litigant は「訴訟当事者」。

[*p.*54 *l.*21] **frivolous**:ここでは「(訴えなどが) 根拠のない」。「軽薄な」「不真面目な」「分別のない」「くだらない」などの意味もある。frivolous girl で「軽薄な娘」、frivolous issue で「取るに足らない問題」となる。

[*p.*55 *l.*8] **squatting**:ここでの squat は「居座る」「不法占拠する」。「しゃがむ」「うずくまる」という意味もあり、上半身を伸ばして行

う膝の屈伸運動は、日本語でも「スクワット」というトレーニング方法として定着している。

[*p.55 l.13*] **harassing**：harass は「嫌がらせをする」「苦しめる」「困らせる」。名詞は harassment で、sexual harassment「セクハラ」、power harassment「パワハラ」、academy harassment「アカハラ」などは、日本でもよく使われるようになっている。

[*p.55 l.17*] **blatant**：ここでは「(ウソなどが) 見え透いた」「わざとらしい」「ずうずうしい」。語源はラテン語の *blatire* (ペらぺらしゃべる)。16世紀末にイングランドの詩人 Edmund Spenser が "The Faerie Queene"「妖精の女王」という作品の中で Blatant Beast という造語を使い、一般的になった。これは「100枚の舌と1本の毒牙を持った化け物」で、「中傷」「悪口」を擬人化したもの。

[*p.55 l.23*] **accounting**：「会計学」。「経理」「計算法」「決算」などの意味もある。accounting year は「会計年度」。

[*p.56 l.7*] **if something is too good to be true, it usually is.**：「話がうますぎるときは、だいたいウソである」。too good to be true だけでも「話がうますぎる」「眉唾ものだ」という意味になる。

[*p.57 l.10*] **plain**：「美しくない」「不美人の」。ここでは ugly「醜い」の婉曲表現として使用されている。類語に homely がある。これはアメリカでは「不器量な」という意味だが、英国では「家庭的な」「素朴な」「質素な」というニュアンスが強い。

[*p.57 l.10*] **pebble-thick glasses**：「ぶ厚いレンズのめがね」。日本でよく使う表現では「牛乳ビンの底のようなめがね」。pebble は「小石」のことだが、「水晶レンズ」「度の強いレンズ」という意味もある。

One Man's Meat Is Another Man's Poison

[*p.58 タイトル*] **One Man's Meat Is Another Man's Poison**：「甲の薬は乙の毒」。ある者の肉は他の者には毒、すなわち、好ましいものは人によって異なるという意味のことわざ。

[*p.58 l.1*] **Jews**：「ユダヤ人、ユダヤ教徒」。Jew の形容詞形は Jewish で、Jewish pianist なら「ユダヤ人ピアニスト」。ちなみに Jew の語源は Judah で、聖書「創世記」にあるヤコブの子「ユダ」と彼が始祖とされる古代の「ユダ王国」のこと。現代でも Judah は男性の名前として使われ、愛称は Jude (英国出身の俳優 Jude Law でおなじみ)。女性形は Judith で、愛称は Judy、Jude。キリストを裏切ったイスカリオテの「ユダ」は Judas。

[*p.58 l.2*] **Muslims**：「イスラム教徒」。形容詞の Muslim は「イスラム教の、イスラムの」。Muslim countries と言えば「イスラム教の国々」。アラビア語から入った言葉で、意味は a person who submits「服従する者」、すなわち神アラーに従う人。

[*p.58 l.2*] **the calls to prayer, emanating from the mosques**：「モスクから流れる礼拝時告知」。call は「呼びかけ」、prayer は「祈り、礼拝」、emanate は「(音や光が) 発する」、mosque は「モスク」。

[*p.58 l.4*] **decibels**：「デシベル」。「deci (1/10) + bel (電力や音の

大きさを表す単位)」からなる。この bel は電話の発明者 Alexander Graham Bell からきたもの。

[p.58 l.6] **minarets**:「ミナレット、光塔」。モスクのドームのそばにそびえる細長い塔。

[p.58 l.6] **azans**: azan / adhan は「アザーン、礼拝時告知」。日に5回の礼拝が義務づけられており、場所と時期によって礼拝の時刻は毎日変わる。それぞれの時間に礼拝をするよう呼びかける朗唱がアザーン。朝一番の礼拝は明け方から日の出までの間に行う。

[p.58 l.7] **the faithful**: faithful は「(人・組織・信仰に) 忠実な、信心深い」で、faith (~への強い信頼、信仰) + -ful (~でいっぱいの)という成り立ち。「the +形容詞」で「~な人々」を表し、the faithful は「信徒、教徒」「(政党や主義などの) 信奉者」。

[p.58 l.11] **Israeli**:「イスラエルの」「イスラエル人」。Israel「イスラエル」の正式英語名は State of Israel「イスラエル国」。

[p.58 l.12] **is backing a bill banning the use of loudspeakers**:「拡声器の使用を禁じる法案を支持している」。back は動詞で「(人や議論を) 支援する、支持する」。bill は「法案」。ban は「(法律などが~を公式に) 禁止する」。loudspeaker は「スピーカー、拡声器」。

[p.58 l.16] **the ban should be extended to 9 am**:「(使用) 禁止は午前9時まで延長されるべきである」。ban は「禁止 (令)」、extend は「拡大する」「(期限などを) 延ばす」。

[p.58 l.19] **going on**: go on は物事がある期間「続く」こと。

[p.58 l.20] **Since Israel was developed on land that mostly belonged to Muslim Arabs, he has a point.**:「イスラエル国がつくられたのは大部分がイスラム教徒のアラブ人に属する土地なので、彼の言い分には一理ある」。since は「~なので」。develop は「(土地などを) 開発する、造成する」。mostly は副詞で「たいてい、主として」。belong to ... は「~に属する、~の所有物である」。Arab は「アラブ人」。have a point は「言っていることがもっともだ」。

[p.59 l.3] **sympathetic to**:「~に同情的な、~に共感して」。名詞形の sympathy は「同情、思いやり」で、「syn- (「共に」を表す接頭辞) + -pathy (「感情」を表す複合要素)」からなる。

[p.59 l.6] **dominates**:「支配する、多数を占める」

[p.59 l.7] **riotous**:「騒々しい、羽目をはずした」。名詞形の riot は「暴動」。

[p.59 l.9] **Alas for ...**:「ああ、哀れなる~よ」。悲しみや落胆などを表す芝居がかった言い回し。

[p.59 l.11] **booming**: ここでの booming は名詞の前に付く形容詞で、「鳴り響く」「ブームに沸く、好景気の」。boom は「ブーンブーンという音が鳴る、どーんととどろく」といった意味の擬音語で、「(音が) 響き渡る」「景気づく」などの意味も持つ。

[p.59 l.12] **echoing**: echo は「こだまする、反響する」。語源はギリシャ神話の森の精 Echo「エコー」。Narcissus「ナルキッソス」を思って焦がれ死にし、声だけが残った。ナルキッソスも水面に映った自分の姿に恋し、やつれ死んで、水仙となった。

[p.59 l.14]　**couldn't get a wink of sleep**：「一睡もできなかった」。not sleep a wink あるいは not get a wink of sleep は「一睡もしない」という意味の成句。この a wink はウィンクではなく「瞬く間」。

[p.59 l.17]　**imam**：「(イスラム教の集団で行う) 礼拝の導師」

[p.59 l.21]　**Saudi Arabia**：「サウジアラビア」。正式英語国名は Kingdom of Saudi Arabia「サウジアラビア王国」。Saudi は統治するサウード王家を示し、「サウジアラビアの、サウジアラビア人」という意味でも使われる。一大産油国サウジアラビアは政教一致の国で、イスラム教の最大勢力 Sunni「スンニ派」の大擁護者。

[p.59 l.22]　**invested in**：invest in ... は「〜に投資する、〜を買う」。invest は in (中に) + vest (衣類を着せる)。investment は「投資」、investor は「投資家」。

[p.60 l.2]　**prevail**：「(習慣や状態が) 広く行き渡っている、普及している」という意味だが、ここでは「幅を利かせている」というニュアンス。

[p.60 l.8]　**banks**：「両岸」。この bank は「土手、岸」。「銀行」の bank は両替商の「勘定台」を意味するイタリア語 banco が語源と言われる。その2つには一段高くなったところという共通イメージがあり、あながち単なる同音異義語ではないとの説もある。

[p.60 l.8]　**dramatize the exotic desert landscape**：「エキゾチックな砂漠の風景をいっそうドラマチックに見せている」。dramatize は「劇化する、脚色する」、exotic は「異国情緒の」、desert は「砂漠」(ちなみに「デザート」は dessert)、landscape は「(一望のもとに広がる) 風景、景色」。

[p.60 l.11]　**melodious**：「旋律が美しい、音楽的な」。名詞形は melody「メロディー、旋律」。

[p.60 l.23]　**rent**：「家賃、賃貸料」

[p.61 l.2]　**blissfully happy**：「この上なく幸せな」。blissfully は「この上もなく」。blissful だけでも「この上なく幸せな、喜びにあふれた」。

[p.61 l.13]　**with the aid of**：「(人や道具) の助けを借りて」。without the aid of ... なら「〜の助けを借りずに」。

[p.61 l.17]　**endure**：「(苦痛や困難に) 耐える、辛抱する」

[p.61 l.21]　**No wonder**：後ろに文が続き、「〜は不思議ではない」。It's no wonder (that) ... と同様。

[p.62 l.2]　**look before you leap**：Look before you leap. はことわざで、文字どおりには「跳ぶ前には見よ」、すなわち「転ばぬ先の杖」。

[p.62 l.4]　**after being deafened by the church bells**：「教会の鐘の音によって耳がつんざかれんばかりになったあとで」。deafen は「(人を一時的に、あるいはずっと) 耳が聞こえなくする」。通常 be deafened の形で使われる。deaf (耳が聞こえない) + -en (〜にする)。

"Plastic Changed My Life!"

[p.63 l.3]　**plastic surgery**：「整形手術」。plastic は「プラスチック(製の)」だが、「形成力のある」「自由に形を変えることができる」「芸

術的創造力のある」という意味もある。故に性格や心が「柔軟な」「感受性の強い」「感じやすい」から「見せかけの」「うわべだけの」「偽の」と意味が広がり、plastic smile は「作り笑い」となる。最近では「クレジットカード」のことを plastic と言うようになっており、pay with plastic では「クレジットカードで支払う」。また、コンビニやスーパーでもらう「レジ袋」は plastic bag となる。surgery は「外科」「手術」のこと。「外科医」は surgeon となる。

[p.63 l.6] **Tupperware**：米国フロリダ州に本社のある「タッパーウェア社」、および同社が製造・販売する商品のこと。社名は創業者のアール・タッパーに由来。「タッパーウェア」は密封性が高く電子レンジにもかけられるプラスチック製の容器で、商標登録されている。

[p.63 l.6] **manufactures**：manufacture は動詞では「製造する」、名詞では「生産、産業」「製品」という意味になる。語源はラテン語の *manus*（手）に *factura*（作られる）が結合した「手仕事」に由来するが、英語の manufacture は「工場で機械によって大規模に生産する」というニュアンスが強い。「捏造する」という意味もあり、manufacture evidence で「証拠をでっちあげる」、manufactured article で「捏造記事」となる。manufacturer は「製造業者、メーカー」「工場主」。

[p.63 l.7] **containers**：container は「容器」「入れ物」のこと。貨物輸送に用いる大きな箱状の容器を「コンテナ」と呼び、container ship と言えば「コンテナ船」のこと。

[p.63 l.8] **Aside from ...**：「〜は別として」「〜を除いては」「〜に加えて」。aside は「わきに」「離れて」「別にして」という副詞で、joking aside は「冗談はさておき」、put ... aside で「取っておく」「蓄える」「（時間などを）空けておく」「片づける」「一時的に忘れる」という意味になる。

[p.63 l.11] **sturdy**：ここでは物が「硬い」「丈夫な」という意味で、strong よりも硬い語。人が「頑丈な」「丈夫な、精神的に「強い」「しっかりした」という意味でも使われ、He is small but sturdy. で「彼は小柄だけど頑丈だ」、sturdy resistance で「不屈の抵抗」となる。

[p.63 l.13] **wages**：「賃金」。特に時間給や日給、週給などを意味することが多い。minimum wage は「最低賃金」、wage cut で「賃金カット」となる。salary は会社勤めの人に支払われる固定給の「月給」「年俸」を意味し、古代ローマ時代に兵士に与えられた *salārium*（塩を買うための給金）からきている。

[p.63 l.13] **well under 10 US dollars**：「10 米ドルよりかなり下回る」。ここでの well は副詞で「ずいぶん」「相当に」「かなり」という意味で、例えば a sum well over the amount agreed upon「同意した額をはるかに超える金額」、She came home well past midnight.「彼女は夜中の 12 時をだいぶ過ぎてから帰宅した」などのように使うことができる。

[p.64 l.2] **the unthinkable**：「考えられないこと」「思いも寄らぬこと」。「the ＋形容詞」で「〜の人々」「〜なもの」という意味になる。ただ、人については the young は「若者たち」、the rich は

「裕福な人々」というふうに複数形となるが、the strange「不思議なこと」、the unknown「未知なるもの」のように the の後に抽象的な形容詞がくると単数扱いになり、例えば The unexpected *has* happened.「予期しないことが起こった」となる。

- [*p.*64 *l.*6] **commissions**：ここでは「手数料」「歩合」。任務・職権の「委託」「委任」、上からの「命令」「指示」、さらには「委員会」という意味もあり、city commission は「市委員会」となる。
- [*p.*64 *l.*25] **fragile**：ここでは、物が「壊れやすい」「もろい」。人が「かよわい、虚弱な、繊細な」という場合にも使われる。また物や人だけではなく、fragile evidence「不十分な証拠」、fragile happiness「はかない幸せ」のように使うこともできる。
- [*p.*65 *l.*3] **smash it to the floor**：「それを床にたたきつける」。smash は「壊す」のほかに「衝突する」「殴る」「強く打つ」「破る」といった意味もあり、A truck smashed against a bus. で「トラックがバスに衝突した」、smash A in the face は「A（人）の顔を殴る」、野球で smash a home run「ホームランを打つ」、smash the enemy で「敵を破る」のように使用される。名詞では、テニスやバドミントンで上からボールを強打する smash「スマッシュ」、さらには smash musical show「大当たりのミュージカル」、smash hit「スマッシュヒット」のように「大成功」という意味でも使われる。
- [*p.*65 *l.*5] **scratch**：「かすり傷」。動詞では「引っかく」「こする」「かゆいところをかく」となる。from scratch という口語表現は「最初から、ゼロから」。この scratch は「地面を引っかいて引いたスタートライン」のこと。
- [*p.*65 *l.*8] **childproof**：「子供にも安全な」「子供の乱暴な扱いに耐える」。-proof は「〜を防ぐ」「〜に耐える」、あるいは「〜に安全な」「〜にも扱える」という意味の接尾辞。waterproof は「防水の」、fireproof は「耐火性のある」、bulletproof は「防弾の」。
- [*p.*65 *l.*11] **dire**：ここでは「悲惨な」「切迫した」。ほかにも「恐ろしい」「ものすごい」「不吉な」という意味もある。語源はラテン語の *dīrus*(恐ろしい、不吉な、不運な)。
- [*p.*65 *l.*15] **for the sake of**：「(目的や利益) のために」。sake は「目的」「理由」「利益」。because of ... も「〜のために」と訳されるが、これは原因や理由を表す場合に使用される。
- [*p.*65 *l.*20] **turned into**：turn into は「〜に変わる」。人や物の性質や外見などが「変化する、変わる、別の状態に「変化させる、変える」という意味で、turn water into ice「水を氷に変える」、turn the stock into cash「株を現金に換える」などのように使うことができる。
- [*p.*66 *l.*8] **commonplace**：形容詞で「普通の」「平凡な」「ありふれた」。「陳腐な」「つまらない」という意味もあり、commonplace remark で「陳腐な言葉」となる。common も「普通の」「ありふれた」だが、もともと「共通の」という意味で、それが「広く行き渡った」「一般的な」から「普通の」となった。
- [*p.*66 *l.*14] **account executive**：「顧客担当責任者」。広告代理店な

どで、会社を代表して特定の取引先とやり取りをし、専門的助言など必要な業務サービスを行うスタッフのこと。

[p.66 l.15] **to further my ambition**:「私の野心をさらに満たすために」。広告業界で成功を収めたいという野望を少しでも現実に近づけようとする著者の気持ちがこの表現に込められている。further は通常「もっと遠くへ、なおいっそう、さらに」という副詞や「もっと遠い」「さらにいっそうの」といった形容詞で使われるが、ここでは動詞で「進める、促進する」という意味。ambition は「野心」「野望」「大志」。形容詞は ambitious「野心的な、大志を抱いた、功名心に燃えて」で、Boys, be ambitious!「少年よ、大志を抱け」は、アメリカ人のクラーク博士が札幌農学校（現・北海道大学）を去るときに教え子に贈った言葉として有名。語源はラテン語の *ambitiōn*（町を歩き回って自分に投票するように訴えること）で、そこから「名誉欲、野望」という意味になった。

[p.66 l.17] **the Vatican of advertising**:「広告界のバチカン」。Vatican はローマ教皇庁「バチカン宮殿」のことで、カトリック教会の総本山であることから、著者は「中心地」「憧れの地」という意味で使っている。advertising は名詞で「広告」、advertisement とも言う。動詞は advertise「広告する、宣伝する」。

[p.67 l.3] **prior to ...**：ここでは「～より前に」「～に先立って」。「優先して」という意味もある。prior は「前の、先の、優先する」。

[p.68 l.2] **demurred**：demur は「返事をしぶる」「躊躇する」「ためらう」という意味の文語的表現。

[p.68 l.5] **snapped back**：ここでの snap back は「きつく言い返す」。snap は「パチン」「ピシッ」「カチッ」という擬音から生まれた単語で、動詞では「パチンと鳴らす」「パタンと閉まる」「ポキンと折れる」などとなる。そこから「素早く動く」「鋭い口調で言う」というふうに意味が広がった。

[p.68 l.8] **take it or leave it NOW**：「仕事をするのか、しないのか今すぐ決めろ！」。この文では「嫌ならやめろ！」という相手の"上から目線"を感じる。命令文か you can、I can を伴って、「申し出を受けるかどうかは勝手で、どちらでもいい」というニュアンスの表現。

[p.68 l.10] **Greyhound**：「グレイハウンド」。膨大な数と運行距離の路線を誇るアメリカ最大のバス会社。同社の長距離バスそのものも指す。社名はドッグレースで最も速く走る狩猟犬「グレイハウンド」に由来し、バスのボディにはこの犬の絵が描かれている。

[p.68 l.21] **on a door-to-door basis**：「ドアからドアを訪問するという方法で」。door-to-door は「戸別の」、basis は「原則」「基準」という意味で、電話や DM などでセールスするのではなく、家を一軒ずつ訪ねるという原則でセールスをしたという意味。on ... basis を使った表現には、ほかに on a priority basis「優先順で」、on a commission basis は「歩合制で」、on a fifty-fifty basis「半々で」、on a gold basis「金本位制で」、あるいは「早く来た人から先に」という原則の on a first-come-first-served basis「先着順で」「早

い者勝ちで」などがある。

[p.68 l.23] **rung**：もともと「はしごの段・横棒」のことで、そこから地位などの「段階」「ランク」の意味になった。start at the bottom rung で「どん底からたたき上げる」、on the top rung は「絶頂に、最高の段階に」という意味になる。

[p.68 l.23] **employment totem pole**：「雇用のトーテムポール」。トーテムポールは北米のネイティブアメリカンが像を彫って彩色を施した木の柱のことで、上下に像が並ぶことから「階層組織、階層制」という意味でも使われるようになった。

[p.69 l.4] **arming myself with a sales kit**：「販売キットで武装して」。arm A with は「Aを〜で武装する、武装させる」。ラテン語の *arma*（武器）に由来する。セールスの大変さを戦争の用語を使って大げさに表現している。sales kit は「販売するための一式、ひとそろいの道具」のこと。

[p.69 l.7] **banging**：bang は「ドンドンたたく、ノックする」。bang は「バンバン、ドンドン、バタン」という擬音で、動詞では「打つ」「たたく」「銃を撃つ／放つ」という意味になる。

[p.69 l.10] **slammed**：「ドアをピシャリと閉めた」。slam はもともと「バタン、ピシャリ」という音のことで、ドアや窓などを「バタンと閉める」、物を「ガチャン／ドシンと置く」、野球で「ホームランを打つ」などの意味がある。名詞では「完勝」「大成功」という意味もあり、grand slam は野球では「満塁ホームラン」、テニスやゴルフではひとりの選手が1シーズンに主要な大会すべてで優勝することになる。

[p.69 l.11] **couldn't stand any more**：「これ以上我慢できなかった」。ここでの stand は「我慢する」「耐える」。通常、否定文で can't や couldn't を伴って使用される。any more は通常、否定文で「もはや〜でない」という意味で使われる。

[p.69 l.12] **CEO**：chief executive officer「最高経営責任者」の略。会社のすべての業務を統括する役員のこと。ちなみに COO（chief operating officer）は「最高執行責任者」、CFO（chief financial officer）は「最高財務責任者」。

[p.69 l.20] **damn well**：「ちゃんと」「確かに」という意味の俗語表現。

[p.69 l.22] **charity organization**：「慈善団体」。charity には「慈善（行為）」「チャリティー」のほかに、「慈悲」「思いやり」「寛容」「隣人愛」といった意味もある。語源はラテン語の *cāritās*（愛すべき）。

[p.70 l.13] **On top of that**：「その上さらに」「それに加えて」「そのほかには」。in addition to that と言い換えることもできる。

[p.70 l.16] **human nature**：「人間性」「人の性」「人情」。human は名詞で「人、人間」、形容詞では「人間の」「人間らしい」。nature は「自然」のことだが、ここでは「本質」「本性」、つまり「本来のありのままの姿」のこと。

From Dog Meat to Crufts Champion

[p.71 l.2] **mongrel**：形容詞で「雑種の」。名詞では「雑種（犬）」と

いう意味にもなる。中期英語の *gemang*（混合物）に由来する。動詞は mongrelize「雑種にする」「交配する」。ちなみに「猫の雑種」は moggie（moggy）と言う。

[*p.71 l.3*] **stray**：形容詞で「はぐれた」「道に迷った」。聖書には stray sheep「迷える子羊」が「人々」「キリスト教信者」という意味で登場する。名詞では「野良犬、野良猫」などとなるが、人の「迷子」という意味にもなる（stray child と言うこともある）。stray は動詞では「はぐれる」「迷い込む」だが、「それる」「逸脱する」という意味もあり、Don't stray from the point. とすると「要点からそれてはいけない」ということになる。

[*p.71 l.4*] **sniffing for scraps**：sniff for scrap は「残飯をあさる」。sniff は「鼻で匂いをクンクンかぐ」だが、さらに「鼻であしらう」「バカにする」という意味もある。scrap は「かけら」「断片」「（鉄くずや切り抜きの）スクラップ」だが、この文脈のように複数形になると「残飯」「食べ残し」という意味になる。

[*p.71 l.6*] **Crufts Dog Show**：「クラフツ・ドッグショー」。イギリスのバーミンガムで毎年開催されるケンネルクラブ主催のドッグショーのこと。世界最大としてギネスブックにも記載されている。犬用ビスケットを売る業者であった Charles Cruft 氏が始めた大会で、ビクトリア朝時代の 1891 年から続く長い歴史を持つ。大会の目玉は、まず犬種や性別、年齢ごとに最も血統が良く健康な犬が選ばれ、最終的に全犬種の代表が優勝を競うという「ベスト・イン・ショー」。そのほかにも、障害物競争やダンス競技、レスキュー犬や警察犬、猟犬などの「働く犬」、あるいは人との感動秘話を持つ「ヒーロー犬」が対象の審査などが行われる。

[*p.71 l.7*] **seemingly impossible transformation take place**：「ちょっと考えてみると、あり得ないほどの変化が起こった」。seemingly は「うわべは」「表面上は」「見たところ、聞いたところでは」という意味の副詞で、She's seemingly cold, but actually quite warm-hearted. と言えば「彼女は見たところ冷たそうだが、実際は温かい心の持ち主だ」という意味になる。transformation は「変化」「転換」で、野良犬がドッグショーで優勝するという「大きな変わりよう」を意味している。take place は「（事件などが）起こる」「行われる」という意味。例えば、The battle took place 70 years ago. で「70 年前に戦争が起こった」、The Olympic Games will take place in Tokyo in 2020. なら「2020 年に東京でオリンピックが開かれる」となる。

[*p.71 l.11*] **lifespan**：「（生き物の）寿命」。物や会社などの「存続期間」という場合にも使用される。life-span、life span とも表記する。「平均寿命」は average lifespan、あるいは average life expectancy とも言う。

[*p.71 l.15*] **relish the thought of eating 'dog meat stew'**：「犬の肉入りシチューを楽しみにしている」。relish は「（食べ物を）おいしく味わう、賞味する」「たしなむ」「楽しむ」、relish the thought of doing で「～したいと思う」「～することを望んでいる」という

意味になる。relish は名詞になると「(食材特有の)風味」「美味」「持ち味」「面白み」。

[p.71 l.20] **bear paws**:「熊の手」。paw は正確に言うと「動物の爪 (claw) と肉趾 (pad) を含む手足の部分」のこと。

[p.72 l.4] **do with**:「扱う」

[p.72 l.5] **slung**:sling「放り投げる」の過去形。sling には「投石器で石を投げる、飛ばす」「(つり革で) つるす」という意味もある。もともと名詞で「投石器」、あるいは旧約聖書「サムエル記」で羊飼いのダビデが大男のゴリアテを倒した「パチンコ」などのことを言った。

[p.72 l.7] **Soi Dog Foundation**:「ソイ・ドッグ・ファウンデーション」。タイで犬や猫の動物福祉向上に活動する団体のこと。動物虐待の抑止や迷い犬や野良猫に飼い主を見つけることなどにより、「動物と人間のより良い共同体の創造」を活動目的とする。

[p.72 l.8] **abandoned**:「見捨てられた」「放棄された」。動詞 abandon は「見捨てる」「(途中で計画などを) やめる」、さらに「断念する」「放棄する」などの意味もある。

[p.72 l.10] **took a flash photo of**:「~をフラッシュ撮影した」。take a photo of ... で「~を撮影する」。

[p.72 l.21] **nurse him back to health**:「元気になるまで / 健康を取り戻すまで、彼を看病する」。nurse は名詞では「看護師」「看護人」「保母」のこと。動詞では「看病する」「介抱する」「授乳する」「大切に育てる」「運用管理する」などとなる。

[p.72 l.23] **recovered**:ここでの recover は「(病気から) 回復する」。「正常な状態に戻す」「埋め合わせる」などの意味もある。recover one's health で「(人が) 健康を回復する、取り戻す」。

[p.72 l.25] **posted his picture on their Facebook**:「彼らのフェイスブックに (犬の) 写真を載せた」。post は「(公共の場に) 掲示する」「(ポスターを) 貼る」などの意味があるが、最近では「情報・メッセージをインターネット上に掲載 / 掲示 / 投稿する」という意味でも使われている。

[p.73 l.2] **adopt**:動詞で「養子にする」という意味だが、ここでは「ペットとして飼う」ということ。ほかにも「採用する」「可決する」「(習慣を) 身に付ける」「(態度を) とる」「(名前を) 選ぶ」という意味でも使われる。

[p.73 l.4] **autism**:「自閉症」

[p.73 l.10] **take to**:この文脈では「なじむ」「なつく」「好きになる」。ほかには「没頭する、専念する」「手段を取る」という意味もある。

[p.73 l.14] **led a sad and solitary existence**:「悲しく孤独な暮らしを送っていた」。led は lead の過去形で、通常「導く」「率いる」「連れていく」という意味を思い浮かべるが、「(人生を) 送る、(時間を) 過ごす」という意味もある。existence には「存在」「実在」のほかにも、この文脈のように「生活」「暮らしぶり」という意味もあり、He led a peaceful existence. で「彼は幸せに満ちた生活を送った」となる。

[p.74 l.3] **stroke**:動詞で「優しくなでる、さする」。もうひとつ別の

語源から生まれた stroke という単語もあるが、これは「打撃、一撃」「一筆」「脳卒中、発作」「ボートのオールのひと漕ぎ」などの意味。

[p.74 l.7] **shower him with kisses**：「彼へキスのシャワーを浴びせる」。shower with ... は「〜を大いに与える、惜しみなく注ぐ」という意味。

[p.74 l.10] **solace**：悲しみや苦悩を和らげる「慰め」「癒やし」「安堵」。例えば The soldier found solace in looking at pictures of his family. で「兵士は家族の写真を見ることに慰めを見いだした」となる。

[p.74 l.10] **in abundance**：「大量に」「豊富に」。abundance には「多量」「多数」のほかに、「(あふれるような) 豊かさ」「(生活の) 裕福さ」という意味もある。

[p.74 l.19] **enter ... as a contestant**：「出場者として〜の参加申し込みをする」。enter には「入る」のほかに、試合や試験に「参加 (登録) する」「申し込む」という意味がある。contestant はコンテストやコンクールの「参加者」「出場者」「競争者」で、ラテン語の *contestari* (証人として呼ぶ) を語源とする。

[p.74 l.24] **pedigrees going back years**：「何代もさかのぼる血統」「何年も前からある血統」。pedigree は「(動物の) 血統書」「血統」。語源は中期フランス語の *pie de grue* (ツルの脚) で、系図の線をツルの脚に見立てた表現。人の「家系図」も family pedigree と言う場合がある。また pedigree には「古い立派な家系、名門」という意味もあり、family of pedigree は「旧家、名門」の意味。「家系図」には genealogy という単語もあり、family tree とも言う。これも「ツルの脚」と同じように「系図」の線を木の枝にたとえた表現。go back years は「何年も昔からある」「何代もさかのぼる」という意味で、その犬の血統が何代も登録されていることを表している。

[p.75 l.1] **'Crufts Friends for Life' award**：クラフツ・ドッグショーのコンテスト種目のひとつで、人の親友としての犬をたたえるための賞。犬と飼い主の心温まるエピソードが紹介され、最も感動的な物語を持った犬が優勝する。

[p.75 l.11] **formalities**：複数形では「(一連の正式な) 手続き」を指す。ここでは competitive formalities なので、チャンピオン犬を決めるまでのいろいろな「審査」のこと。

[p.75 l.12] **finalists**：「決勝戦進出選手/チーム」のこと。「決勝戦」という意味の final に、「〜する人」という接尾辞 -ist が付属した言葉。

[p.75 l.16] **A friend in need is a friend indeed.**：「まさかのときの友こそ真の友」。「苦しいとき、困ったときに、そばにいてくれる友達は本当の友達だ」という意味のことわざ。in need と indeed が韻を踏んでいる。昔から知られた古いことわざで、紀元前3世紀に活躍した共和政ローマ時代の詩人クイントゥス・エンニウスの作品にもこの表現が見られる。

[p.75 l.22] **have many uses**：「多くの使い道がある」。この use は名詞で「使用法」「用途」「利用法」「使用目的」などの意味がある。

[p.75 l.24] **smuggle**：「密輸入/密輸出する」「こっそり持ち運ぶ」。「運び屋」「密輸入者、密輸出者」、「密輸船」は smuggler と言う。

[p.76 l.5] **strenuous**：形容詞で「骨の折れる」「激しい」「難しい」。strenuous opposition で「激しい反対」、make strenuous efforts で「大いに奮励努力する」などとなる。

[p.77 l.3] **tarmac**：ここでは「滑走路」のこと。「タールマック」とは舗装用アスファルト凝結剤の商品名。そこから滑走路や道路や駐車場などタールマックで舗装された場所のことも、そう呼ぶようになった。もともとは tarmacadam（タールマカダム）と言った。これは tar「タール」とこの舗装材の発明者、J. L. McAdam の名前を組み合わせた造語。

[p.77 l.5] **Alsatian dogs**：「ジャーマンシェパード」。ドイツ原産にもかかわらず第2次世界大戦後の反独感情から、ドイツに隣接するフランスのアルザス地方に由来して Alsatian（アルザス種）と呼ばれる。Alsatian は「アルザス人」「アルザス地方の」という意味。

[p.77 l.10] **from Ecuador to Cuba and thence to Miami**：「エクアドルからキューバへ、そこからマイアミへ」。thence は「そこから」という意味の文語的な副詞。場所の移動だけなく時間的な移り変わり、因果関係などに関しても使い、「そのときから」「その結果」「それがもとで」という意味もある。例えば She fell ill and thence was seldom seen. で「彼女は病気になり、それからめったに姿を見せなくなった」。

[p.77 l.18] **emptied out**：empty out は「中身を残らず出して空にする」。empty は「空の」という形容詞だが、動詞では「空にする」「空ける」という意味になる。

[p.77 l.21] **PLANT drugs on me**：「私が麻薬を持っているように仕組む」。plant は名詞で「植物、草木」、動詞で「植える、種をまく」だが、そのほかに「（人をあざむくために）置いておく、ひそかに仕掛ける」という意味もある。

Insect Burger, Anyone?

[p.79 l.1] **The very thought of eating an insect, even touching one**：「昆虫を食べることなんて、触ることでさえ、ちょっと考えただけでも」。ここでの very は形容詞で「ほんの〜」。

[p.79 l.2] **disgusting**：「気分が悪くなる（ような）」

[p.79 l.6] **bugs**：「虫」。bug は insect よりくだけた表現で、クモ、ダニなど昆虫でないものも含まれる。日本語の「虫」に「マニア、愛好者」の意味があるように、英語にも be bitten by the ... bug「〜の虫に刺される」から「〜にハマっている」といった表現がある。

[p.79 l.9] **hygienic**：「衛生的な」。名詞形は hygiene「衛生」。

[p.79 l.10] **The fact is, ...**：「実は〜だ」。信じがたいことや意外なことを切り出すときに使われる表現。... の部分には普通の文（主語＋動詞）がくる。

[p.79 l.10] **gourmet dishes**：「グルメ料理」。gourmet は「美食家、グルメ」「食通の、美味の」。dish は「料理」。

[p.79 l.11] **upmarket**：イギリス英語で「高級な、ハイソ向けの」。ア

メリカ英語では upscale がよく使われる。
- [p.79 l.14] **patrons**:「パトロン、常連客、ひいき客」
- [p.79 l.15] **I MUST have an INSECT Burger!**:「昆虫バーガーを食べさせろ！」。この must は「～せねばならならない」という義務というよりは「どうしても～したい」という固執を表す。
- [p.79 l.16] **get over ...**:「(問題など)を克服する、(恐怖など)を抑える」
- [p.79 l.17] **negative attitude**:「否定的態度、拒否反応」
- [p.79 l.20] **eschewed**: eschew は硬い語で「(好ましくないものや有害なものを意識的に) 避ける、控える」。
- [p.80 l.6] **scallops topped with bamboo EARTHWORMS**:「ホタテの竹虫のせ」。scallop は「ホタテ貝」。topped with は「～を上に載せた、トッピングした」。bamboo earthworm は竹の中にいて「竹虫」と通称される、タケツトガなどの幼虫。earthworm は「ミミズ」だが、チョウやガの幼虫なども指す。
- [p.80 l.7] **fish in ANT sauce**:「アリソースをかけた魚」。ant は「アリ」。刺されると危険な「ヒアリ」は a fire ant。
- [p.80 l.9] **I've been won over.**:「すっかり気に入った」。win A over は「A を味方に引き入れる、A の心をつかむ」。ここでは受身形になっている。
- [p.80 l.11] **locusts**:「イナゴ、バッタ」。広くバッタを指すが、特に大群で移動して農作物を食い荒らすダイミョウバッタ (migratory locust) のイメージが強い。
- [p.80 l.11] **has been appreciated**:「味わわれてきた」
- [p.80 l.17] **preconceptions**: preconception は「先入観、偏見」。複数形で使われることも多い。
- [p.80 l.24] **congratulated**:「絶賛した」。congratulate は「祝う」「称賛する」。おなじみ Congratulations!「おめでとう！」の動詞形。
- [p.81 l.2] **RAT**: rat は「ネズミ」。mouse「ハツカネズミ、マウス」より大型のドブネズミやクマネズミの類。
- [p.81 l.9] **wherever it comes from**:「そのネズミがどこからやって来ようと」。wherever は「どこであれ」。
- [p.81 l.12] **skull**:「頭蓋骨」
- [p.81 l.17] **white lie**:「悪意のないウソ」。方便でついたウソ。
- [p.81 l.17] **he does have a point**:「彼の言葉は実にもっともである」。does have は普通 has と言うところを強調した表現。have a point は「発言に一種の道理がある」。
- [p.81 l.20] **incident**:「(不愉快な) 出来事」
- [p.81 l.23] **lobster thermidor**:「ロブスターのテルミドール」。lobster ははさみの大きな「ロブスター、オマールエビ」、または「イセエビ」。thermidor「テルミドール」は縦半分に割ったエビの殻に身を切ったものを詰めてクリームソースなどをかけてオーブンで焼いた料理。Thermidor はもともとフランス革命暦の第 11 月 (7 月 19 日～ 8 月 17 日) の「熱月」。「テルミドール 9 日のクーデター」(1794 年 7 月 27 日) で、独裁的権力を握っていたロベスピエールが穏健共和派らに倒された。1894 年、当時、劇場のこけら落としにかけら

れていた芝居のタイトルから thermidor が取られ、有名レストランのメニューに命名されたものとも言われる。

[p.81 *l*.23] **complimented**：compliment は「(人を) 褒める」。

[p.81 *l*.24] **signature dish**：「特製料理、自慢料理」。signature dish はいわば、その料理人や店の signature「署名」付きの、つまり太鼓判を押した、オススメ料理、看板メニュー。

[p.82 *l*.4] **scavengers**：scavenger は、ハゲタカやジャッカル、甲虫、甲殻類などで、腐肉や腐敗物を食べる「清掃動物」。「ゴミ箱をあさる人」も指す。元は「道路掃除人」を意味する語が、中期英語で *scavager*「税関検査官」となったものが語源。輸入品をごそごそ探し回るところからきていると言われる。

[p.82 *l*.5] **rubbish**：rubbish はイギリス英語で「(身の回りの) くず、ゴミ、くだらないもの」。アメリカ英語の garbage「(特に生ゴミなどの) ゴミ」や trash「(特に紙くずや段ボールなどの) ゴミ」を含む。

[p.82 *l*.13] **ingesting**：ingest は硬い語で「(食物・薬品を) 摂取する」。-gest は「運ぶ」で、関連する語に egest「(未消化物を)排出・排泄する」(e-「外へ」)、digest「消化する」(di-「別々に」) がある。

[p.83 *l*.4] **vigorous**：「(運動などが) 激しい、(活動・発言などが) 猛烈な、熱烈な」。多大なエネルギーと熱意で事に当たる様子。

[p.83 *l*.5] **dietary habits**：「食習慣」。dietary は「(栄養面から見た) 食事の」。habit は「習慣、癖」。

[p.83 *l*.8] **reckoned**：reckon は「～であると思う、推測する、計算する」。主にイギリス英語でよく使われる。

[p.83 *l*.15] **half-starving**：「半分餓死しそうな」。starving は形容詞で「飢えている、(口語で)腹ぺこな」。動詞形は starve「餓死させる・餓死する、飢え(させ)る、(口語で)腹ぺこである」。

[p.83 *l*.21] **edible**：「食べられる、食用に適した」

[p.83 *l*.23] **larvae**：larva「幼虫、(オタマジャクシなどの) 幼生」の複数形。

[p.83 *l*.24] **nutrition**：「栄養素、栄養のある食物」

[p.84 *l*.4] **insect diet**：「昆虫の入った食べ物」「昆虫食」

[p.84 *l*.4] **bonus**：「プラス、思いがけない余禄 (もうけもの)、有益なもの」

[p.84 *l*.6] **why don't we ...?**：「我々もしたらいいじゃないか」。「なぜしないのか？」という疑問文の形を取った反語表現 (修辞疑問文)。

[p.84 *l*.15] **Vodka**：「ウオッカ」

[p.84 *l*.16] **steeping**：steep は「(液体などに食べ物を) つける・つかっている、浸す・浸っている」。

Will Elephants Completely Disappear in 20 Years' Time?

[p.85 *l*.3] **indiscriminate**：「無差別の」「見境のない」「めちゃくちゃな」という意味の形容詞。「無差別攻撃」のことを indiscriminate attack、「乱読」を indiscriminate reading と言う。反対語の

discriminate は「差別する」という動詞でよく使用されるが、「識別する」という意味もあり、形容詞では「注意深く識別する」という意味にもなる。

[p.85 l.4] **rhinos**：rhino は rhinoceros（動物のサイ）の短縮形。口語では rhino と言うことが多い。語源はギリシャ語の *rhinokerōs* で、rhino は「鼻」、*kerōs* は「角」。ちなみに「鼻科学」のことを rhinology と言う。

[p.85 l.6] **ivory tusks**：「象の牙」。ivory は「象牙」、tusk は「象やイノシシなどの牙」。犬やオオカミ、蛇などの牙は fang と言う。

[p.85 l.7] **horns**：horn は「（ウシ、シカ、ヤギなどの）角」のこと。また、カタツムリなどの「触角」も意味する。ちなみに金管楽器の「ホルン」も、ここからきている。

[p.85 l.9] **Premeditated**：「前もって考えた」「計画的な」。premeditated killing / murder は「計画的殺人」のこと。meditate「沈思黙考する」「もくろむ、計画する」の前に、「前 / 先 / 事前に」を意味する接頭辞 pre- が付いた表現。

[p.85 l.15] **extinct**：「（生命や動物などが）死に絶えた / 絶滅した」という意味の形容詞。火や希望が「消えた」、制度や官職などが「廃止された」、家系や爵位などが「断絶した」、習慣などが「廃れた」という意味でも使われる。「火山が活動をやめた」という意味もあり、「死火山」を extinct volcano と言う。動詞は extinguish「消す / 絶滅させる」。

[p.85 l.16] **dinosaurs**：dinosaur は「恐竜」のこと。「時代遅れの人 / 物」という意味もある。ギリシャ語の *deinōs*（恐ろしい）と *saúra*（トカゲ）の合成語。1842 年にイギリスの解剖学者、リチャード・オーウェンが初めて使用したと言われる。

[p.86 l.1] **reservations**：reservation は「予約」や「指定」だが、「特別保留地」「保護区」という意味もある。ここでは「野生動物の保護区」のこと。

[p.86 l.2] **dwindling**：dwindle は「次第に減少する」「だんだん小さくなる」。また、人が「やせ細る」、名声などが「衰える」、品質が「低下する」という意味でも使用される。

[p.86 l.4] **poachers**：poacher は「密猟者」「密漁者」。動詞は poach「密猟 / 密漁する」。ほかに、他人の土地に「侵入する」「荒らす」、他人の権利などを「侵害する」という意味もある。

[p.86 l.7] **spotted**：動詞の spot は「（苦労して）見つける」「所在を突きとめる」という意味。

[p.86 l.9] **Meanwhile**：「同時に」。「一方では」「その間」「そうしている間に」という意味もある。

[p.86 l.14] **criminal gangs**：「犯罪組織」。criminal は「犯罪的な」、gang は「（悪人や犯罪者の）一団」「暴力団」のこと。「非行グループ」という意味もある。日本では「ギャング」というと「反社会的組織」だけを思い浮かべがちだが、英語では「趣味が同じ仲間」「職場の同僚」という意味もある。

[p.86 l.14] **lucrative**：「もうかる」「金になる」

[*p.86 l.*19] **carvings**:「彫刻」「彫り物」。動詞は carve「彫刻する、彫る」「刻む」。食卓で「肉を切り分ける」という意味もある。

[*p.86 l.*20] **aphrodisiacs**: aphrodisiac とは「催淫薬」「性欲亢進薬」「媚薬」のこと。ギリシャ神話に登場する愛と美と快楽と出生の女神 Aphrodite(アフロディテ)に由来する。その息子とされるのが Eros(エロス)。ローマ神話では Aphrodite が Venus(ビーナス)、Eros は Cupid(キューピッド)となった。

[*p.86 l.*21] **naive**:ここでは「だまされやすい」。考えなどが「世間知らずの」「うぶな」「単純な」という意味でも使用される。日本語で「ナイーブ」というと、「繊細で感受性豊かな」という良いイメージがあるが、英語ではネガティブなニュアンスが強い。

[*p.87 l.*2] **do ... good**:「〜に(薬などが)効く」。do には「(物・事が)利益・害・信用などを(人に)生じさせる / もたらす」、good には「(薬などが)効く」「健康に良い」という意味がある。Change of air will do you good. で「転地なさると体にいいでしょう」、A good night's rest will do you a lot of good. は「夜ぐっすり眠るととても良い効果があります」などと表現できる。

[*p.87 l.*5] **theories**: theory は通常「理論」「説」のことだが、ここでは推量の域を出ない「仮説」のこと。

[*p.87 l.*6] **healing properties**:「効能」。property には「財産」「所有地 / 物」「所有権」などの意味があるが、ここでは「効力」のこと。

[*p.87 l.*7] **hooves**:単数形は hoof、馬などの「ひづめ」のこと。口語で、おどけて「(人の)足」という意味で使用されることもある。

[*p.87 l.*10] **just out of curiosity**:「好奇心から」「興味本位で」。「(好奇心があって)ちょっと聞きたいのですが」という際にも使用され、Just out of curiosity, what happened after that?「ちょっと気になったんだけど、あのあと何があったの?」などと言うことができる。

[*p.87 l.*13] **seahorses**: seahorse は「タツノオトシゴ」のこと。

[*p.87 l.*14] **prize exhibit**:「貴重な陳列品」。prize には形容詞で「賞を得るに値するくらい価値のある」という意味がある。exhibit は名詞では「陳列(品)」「展示(品)」となる。

[*p.88 l.*1] **flesh**:人や動物の「肉」のこと。gain flesh で「太る」、lose flesh で「痩せる」という意味になる。「食肉」の場合には通常 meat を用いる。

[*p.88 l.*6] **Viagra**:「バイアグラ」。1998 年にアメリカで発売された ED (erectile dysfunction)「勃起不全」を治療する医薬品のこと。

[*p.88 l.*16] **bled to death**: bleed to death は「出血多量で死ぬ」。bleed は動詞で「血が出る」「失血する」だが、「ひどく心を痛める」という意味もある。名詞形は blood「血」。

[*p.88 l.*18] **sawn off**: sawn は saw「のこぎりで切る」の過去分詞。saw off は「のこぎりで切り取る」。off は「離れて」というニュアンス。

[*p.88 l.*19] **fenced off**: fence off は、中へ入らせないように「垣根をめぐらせる」。このときはロープなどで、現場に入ることを規制していたものと思われる。

[*p.88 l.*23] **booty**:「戦利品」「略奪品」「獲物」のこと。贈り物・賞品・

謝礼などとして「すばらしいもの」という意味もある。

[p.88 l.25] **prosecute**：「起訴する」「告訴する」

[p.89 l.12] **Spaniards**：「スペイン人」のこと。スペイン国民全体を表す場合は the Spanish。Spanish は名詞では「スペイン人」「スペイン語」、形容詞では「スペインの」「スペイン語の」「スペイン人の」。

[p.89 l.14] **His Majesty**：Majesty は「王族・皇族などに対する敬称」で、His Majesty は「国王陛下」。「女王陛下」は Her Majesty。国王や女王に向かって呼びかけるときは Your Majesty と言う。「両陛下」と言う場合には Their Majesties。日本の「天皇陛下」は His Imperial Majesty、「皇后陛下」は Her Imperial Majesty。呼びかけるときは Your Imperial Majesty となる。王国の「殿下」は His Royal Highness、「妃殿下」は Her Royal Highness、日本の「皇太子殿下」「皇嗣殿下」は His Imperial Highness the Crown Prince、「皇太子妃殿下」「皇嗣妃殿下」は Her Imperial Highness the Crown Princess となる。

[p.89 l.15] **abdicate in favor of ...**：「退位して〜を後継者にする」。abdicate は「(王などが) 退位する」という意味。

[p.89 l.16] **ex-King**：「元国王」。ex- という接頭辞は「元〜」「前〜」という意味で、ex-prime minister「前/元首相」、ex-boyfriend「元カレ」、ex-girlfriend「元カノ」などと言うことができる。

[p.90 l.3] **exquisite netsuke**：「美しい根付」。exquisite は「(技や美しさが) この上なくすばらしい」「優美な」「気品のある」という形容詞。「根付」とは、日本の江戸時代に煙草入れや印籠などを落とさないよう紐で帯からつるす際に使用した留め具のこと。材質は木や象牙などで緻密な彫刻が施されているものも多く、欧米でも芸術品として高く評価されている。多くの美術館で所蔵され、コレクターも多く、根付に関する書籍も数多く発行されている。netsuke は、OED（オクスフォード英語辞典）に収載された、最も古い「日本語」とされている。

[p.90 l.11] **breed**：ここでは「繁殖させる」。ほかに「(子を) 産む」「(家畜を) 飼育する」「育てる」「交配する」などの意味がある。

[p.90 l.16] **harvest**：ここでは動詞で「刈り取る」。ほかには「収穫(する)」「採集 (する)」「捕獲 (する)」「収穫期」「作物」などという意味もある。「秋」を意味する古期・中期英語の *hærfest*、ドイツ語の *Herbst* に由来する。

Why Does "Affluenza" Help Millionaire Killers?

[p.91 タイトル] **Affluenza**：「金持ち病」。「富裕」を意味する affluence と influenza「インフルエンザ」を合わせた言葉。このように2語の一部ずつが合わさってできた語を portmanteau (word)「かばん語」と言う (portmanteau はちょうつがいで2つに分かれるトランク)。brunch (breakfast + lunch) もその例。influenza は「影響」を意味するイタリア語で、もともとは天体の影響によって引き起こされると考えられた「伝染病などの大流行」を指していた。1743年に

イタリアに発した流行性感冒が欧州全体に広がったことから、その流行性感冒を指した influenza が各国語に入った。現在、英語では (the) flu と略して言うことも多い。

[p.91 l.2] **wealthy**：「裕福な」。安定的な財力や影響力があり、地位があることも示唆する。rich は金持ちであることを表す最も一般的な語。財力だけでなく、resource-rich「資源が豊かな」のように何かが普通より豊富にあることも示す。affluent は硬い単語で「富裕な、豊かな」。同じ語源を持つ influx「流入、殺到」のように、よどみない流れのイメージがあり、財力を伸ばし繁栄している人や地域に使われる。

[p.91 l.2] **was finally sentenced to ...**：「ついに〜の判決が下された」。この sentence は動詞で「〜の刑を宣告する」。

[p.91 l.5] **frightful**：主にイギリス英語で使われる形容詞で「恐ろしい」「ひどい」。fright は「突然の恐怖、戦慄」。

[p.91 l.12] **get away with murder**：「好き放題にやっても、おとがめなしで済む」という意味の口語表現。

[p.91 l.13] **defense attorneys**：「被告側弁護人」。defense は「防衛」「守備」「抗弁」「被告側」。attorney のもともとの意味は「任命された人」。「代理人」「弁護士 (attorney-at-law)」「検事 (prosecuting attorney)」といった意味を持つ。類語の lawyer は「弁護士」「法律家」を表す一般的な語。

[p.91 l.19] **lethal carelessness**：「死者が出る不注意」。lethal は「死に至る、致命的な」で、lethal dose なら「(薬などの) 致死量」。メル・ギブソン、ダニー・グローバー主演の映画シリーズ "Lethal Weapon"「リーサル・ウェポン」は文字どおりには「殺人兵器」「凶器」という意味。carelessness は「不注意」「無頓着」。

[p.92 l.9] **Due to this state of mind**：「このような精神状態のため」。due to ... は「〜が原因で」。state of mind は「精神 (mind) の状態 (state)」。ビリー・ジョエルの "New York State of Mind"「ニューヨークの想い」はロサンゼルスを引き払い故郷ニューヨークへ戻ってきたときの心情を歌った名曲。9.11 同時多発テロの追悼の曲としても歌われている。曲名にある New York State は「ニューヨーク州」との掛け言葉にもなっている。

[p.92 l.14] **criminal conduct**：「犯罪行為」。criminal は「犯罪の」「犯罪者」。名詞 conduct は「(道徳上の) 行い、行為」で、アクセントが前にある。動詞では「(調査などを) 行う、管理する」「(楽団などを) 指揮する」。アクセントは後ろ。

[p.92 l.15] **legal circles**：「法曹界、法律家たち」。legal は「法律の」、circles は「仲間、(職業や趣味が同じ人たちの) グループ」。この意味では通常複数形で使われる。political circles なら「政界」、academic circles「学界」、business circles「実業界」となる。

[p.92 l.18] **judge and jury**：「裁判官や陪審員たち」。judge は「裁判官、判事、審判」。語源は「法律を語る人、審理者」。judge と同じくラテン語の *jus*「法律」を語源に持つ語には jurist「法律家」、jurisdiction「司法権、管轄区域」などがある。jury は「誓う人々」

が語源で、意味は「陪審(団)」。juror なら「陪審員」「審査員」。

[p.92 l.20] **An abusive childhood**:「子供のときに虐待を受けたこと」。abusive は「(人が)暴力的な」「(環境などが)虐待のある」。abusive parent なら「虐待する親」。abuse は「乱用(する)」「虐待(する)」。childhood は「幼年期、子供時代」。

[p.92 l.21] **conceivably**:「ひょっとすると」。通例 could などを伴って控えめな推測を表す。動詞 conceive は「con (完全に、一緒に) + ceive ((体内に)取り入れる)」で、「(考えや感情を)抱く、思いつく」「妊娠する」。

[p.92 l.21] **mitigating**:形容詞で「罪を軽減する」。mitigating circumstances なら「酌量すべき情状、軽減事由」。動詞 mitigate は「(苦痛や苦しみなどを)和らげる」「(刑罰などを)軽減する」を意味する硬い表現。

[p.93 l.1] **ought to ...**:「(社会通念的に、期待として)〜すべきだ、〜したほうがいい」。should も同様の意味だが、話者の主観や権威による判断がより示されるという。

[p.93 l.3] **with great wealth comes social responsibility**:倒置になっている文。普通の語順にすると social responsibility comes with great wealth「社会的責任が大きな富とともにやって来る」だが、強調したいことが前に来るので、「大きな富には社会的責任がつきものだ」と捉えたほうが意味が通る。

[p.93 l.5] **deadly**:deadly は「致命的な、死に至る」という意味の形容詞で lethal の類語。deadly terrorist attack「死者が出たテロ事件」「テロ攻撃で死者」のように使われる。

[p.93 l.12] **ended up in the hospital**:「入院するはめになった」。end up ...「最終的に〜になる」。end up in smoke なら「立ち消えになる」。

[p.93 l.14] **Not only did he have three times the legal limit of alcohol in his blood**:「彼は法定血中アルコール濃度の3倍であっただけでなく」。not only「〜だけでなく」に引っ張られて助動詞 did が主語の前に出て、動詞が原形 have で使われる強意表現になっている。飲酒や薬物の影響を受けた運転のことを DUI (driving under the influence) と言う。

[p.93 l.15] **he also tested positive for marijuana and Valium**:「マリファナとバリウムの陽性反応も出た」。also「〜もまた」は文前半の not only と対になるもの。test はここでは「検査の結果が〜である」という意味。positive for ... は「〜が陽性の」。「陰性の」なら negative。marijuana は麻薬の「マリファナ、大麻」。Valium「バリウム」は精神安定剤の名前。胃のレントゲン検査で造影剤として使われる「バリウム」は barium meal と言う。

[p.93 l.17] **Quite a combination**:「大した組み合わせだ」。「quite a / an + 名詞」で「かなりの〜、なかなかの〜」。ここでは間投詞的に使っている。

[p.93 l.19] **cautioned**:動詞 caution は「警告する」。一般的な警告だけでなく、特に警察などが、またやったら次回は罰せられると警

告するときに使われる。名詞の caution は「用心（深さ）」「警告」。caution light なら「注意信号」。形容詞は cautious「用心深い、慎重な」。

[p.93 l.25] **underage**：形容詞で「未成年の」。underage drinking なら「未成年者の飲酒」。「未成年者」は minor と言う。

[p.93 l.25] **he was let off with a caution**：「彼は警告だけで放免された」。let A off は「A（人）を罰しない、釈放する」。

[p.94 l.3] **juvenile institution**：「少年矯正施設」。名詞の juvenile は「（法律用語などの）少年、少女」「児童書」。juvenile delinquency は「少年犯罪、非行」。形容詞では「少年少女向きの」。juvenile books なら「子供向け図書」。institution は「（公共機関・研究機関などの）施設」「療養施設」「協会」など広い意味を持つ語。

[p.94 l.9] **No doubt ...**：「きっと、間違いなく〜」という意味の成句。

[p.94 l.11] **custodial sentence**：「拘束を科す刑」。custodial は形容詞で「拘留の、監禁の」「保護管理の」。名詞の custody は「保護監督権」「親権」の意味でよく使われる。custody battle は「親権争い」。

[p.94 l.18] **plowed into**：plow into ... は「（車が制御不能で人や物に）突っ込む」。plow（イギリス英語では plough）は名詞では「鋤」、動詞では「鋤で耕す」「除雪する」「（船が）波を切って進む」。

[p.94 l.20] **stalled**：この stall は自動詞で「車などが立ち往生する」。名詞では「エンジン停止」「（飛行機の）失速」「屋台」「小さな個室」といった意味があり、「トイレの個室」は toilet stall。

[p.94 l.23] **presided over**：preside over ... で「〜の司会・議長を務める、〜を取り仕切る」。ここでは「裁判長を務める」。

[p.94 l.25] **probation**：「保護観察、執行猶予」。He was put on probation for two years.「彼は2年間の保護観察処分になった」のように使われる。ほかに「試用期間」「仮採用」という意味もある。相応の刑や身分を見極めるための試験的状態を指す語。

[p.95 l.1] **rehabilitation home**：「療養施設」。rehabilitation は「ふさわしくした、能力が備わった」という意味のラテン語 habilitātus が語源。re- は「再び」を表す接頭辞。rehabilitation は「アルコール・薬物などの依存症患者、犯罪者などの社会復帰のための訓練」を主に意味する。略語 rehab もよく使われ、シンガーソングライターのエイミー・ワインハウスがアルコール・薬物依存との苦闘を歌った"Rehab" はグラミー賞3部門を制した（ワインハウスはアルコール中毒のため27歳で死去）。ちなみに病後などの身体の機能回復訓練は physical therapy が一般的。

[p.95 l.6] **offense**：Offense is the best defense.「攻撃は最善の防御である」のように offense は「攻撃」の印象が強いが、ここでは「違反、罪」という意味。

[p.95 l.13] **she threw the book at him**：throw the book at ...「〜に本を投げつける」とは「〜を最大限に厳しく罰する」という意味。この book は膨大な「適用可能法令集、判例集」。

[p.95 l.16] **killing spree**：「殺戮」。spree は「何かを集中的に派手にやること」「ばか騒ぎ」という意味で、spending / shopping spree なら「爆

買い」、spree killer なら「連続殺人犯」。

- [p.95 l.17] **slap-on-the-wrist**：slap on the wrist は「ほんの申し訳の罰(警告)」。ここでは形容詞的に使っている。slap は「平手打ち」、wrist は「手首」。
- [p.95 l.21] **Quite a few psychologists**：quite a few は many と言い換えられる。psychologist は「心理学者」。psych- はギリシャ語由来の「心理、精神」を表す接頭辞。psychiatrist は「精神分析医」。"Psycho" はおなじみヒッチコック監督の映画「サイコ」。
- [p.96 l.8] **mother from hell**：「とんでもない母親」。... from hell は「最低(最悪)の～」という意味のくだけた表現。child from hell なら「悪ガキ」というところだろうか。table from hell は「(レストランで)酔って手に負えない客」「注文のうるさい客」。
- [p.96 l.9] **absconded**：「逃亡した」。abscond は「(容疑者などが)ひそかに逃亡する、行方をくらます」という意味の硬い言葉。言い換えるなら run away。また abscond with money なら「金を持ち逃げする」。abs-(～から離れて)とラテン語の *condere*(置く、据える)からなる。
- [p.97 l.2] **beyond the reach of US law**：「アメリカの法律の手がおよばない」。beyond は「能力や範囲を超えて」という意味。beyond A's control なら「Aの手に負えない」。
- [p.97 l.4] **extradited**：「引き渡された」。extradite は「(本国などへ)犯人や亡命者などを引き渡す、送還する」。ちなみに「犯罪人引き渡し条約」は extradition treaty。
- [p.97 l.18] **plead "Not guilty"**：「"無罪" を主張する」。plead は「申し立てる、主張する」、not guilty は「無罪」。
- [p.97 l.19] **on account of ...**：「～によって、～の理由で」。account には「(原因・理由の)説明」という意味がある。

Did a Ray of Sunshine Reveal Dark Secrets?

- [p.98 タイトル] **a Ray of Sunshine**：「太陽の光」。ray は「光線」。sunshine は「日光、陽光」で、暖かさや明るさ、情報などが日の目を見ることなどのプラスイメージをもつ言葉。a ray of sunshine は「人生を明るくしてくれる人」という比喩にもなる。
- [p.98 l.6] **stressed out**：「ストレスを受けて」。be stressed out は「(人が)ストレスがたまっている、まいっている」。名詞形を使うと be under great stress「大変なストレスを受けている」などと表現できる。
- [p.98 l.9] **reshuffled cabinet**：「改造内閣」。reshuffle は「トランプのカードを切り直す」「人員を入れ替える」。元の動詞 shuffle は「足を引きずって歩く、落ち着きなくもぞもぞ動く」「カードを切る」。cabinet は「内閣」。
- [p.98 l.15] **Cameras ... began clicking**：「(いっせいに)カメラのシャッター音が響いた」。click はインターネットの「クリックする」でおなじみになったが、元は「カチャッと音を立てる、シャッター音

をさせる」。

[*p.*98 *l.*16]　**sunlit**：「太陽に照らされた」。lit は動詞 light「照らす」の過去形・過去分詞。

[*p.*98 *l.*17]　**found their way into the news**：「ニュースネタになることになった」。find one's way into ... は「ひょんなことから〜に現れる、〜の状況になる」。

[*p.*99 *l.*4]　**fuss**：「(不必要な) 大騒ぎ、ひと悶着」

[*p.*99 *l.*12]　**just "making a mountain out of a molehill"**：「『針小棒大に言って騒いでいる』だけ」。make a mountain out of a molehill は文字どおりには「モグラ塚 (molehill) で山をつくる」で、ささいなことを大げさに言うこと。

[*p.*100 *l.*2]　**corruption**：「汚職」

[*p.*100 *l.*4]　**measly**：「ほんのわずかの、たった〜ぽっちの」。「麻疹」は measles と言い、measly には「麻疹にかかった、麻疹の」という意味もある。

[*p.*100 *l.*8]　**the raging battles**：「激しいもみ合い」。raging は「激怒した、猛烈な」。battle は「戦闘、(集団の) 戦い」。タイではタクシン元首相派と反タクシン派が激烈なデモの応酬を繰り返してきた。2014年、その混乱を収拾するとして軍がクーデターを起こして以来、軍主導の暫定政権が続いていた。19 年 7 月、民政のプラユット新首相による政権が発足したが、与野党伯仲の議会、閣僚のスキャンダルなど不安定材料満載での船出となった。

[*p.*100 *l.*15]　**keeps perfect time**：「(時計が) 正確だ、きちんと動く、(人が) 時間を守る」。keep bad time なら「(時計が) 不正確だ、(人が) 時間を守らない」。

[*p.*100 *l.*23]　**stamping out ...**：「〜を根絶すること」。stamp out ... は「(病気や悪習) を根絶する、撤廃する」「火を踏み消す」。「切手、スタンプ」の印象が強い stamp は「粉々に押し砕く」が原義で、動詞としては「ドスンドスン足踏みをする」「スタンプを押す」「刻印する」などの意味を持つ。

[*p.*100 *l.*24]　**TB (tuberculosis)**：「結核」。口語では結核を指して TB がよく使われる。

[*p.*101 *l.*4]　**highly infectious disease**：「感染力の高い病気」。infectious disease は「(間接的感染による) 伝染病」「感染症」。infectious は「(病気などが空気) 感染する」「(人などが病気を) 感染させるおそれがある」「(考えや感情が人に) 伝染しやすい」。disease は「病気、疾患」。a chronic disease なら「慢性疾患」、an acute disease なら「急性疾患」。heart disease は「心臓病」。

[*p.*101 *l.*5]　**diagnosis**：「診断」。make a diagnosis は「診断する」。be diagnosed as ... なら「〜と診断される」。

[*p.*101 *l.*7]　**chemists**：「化学者、薬剤師」。イギリス英語では「薬局、ドラッグストア」も chemist。また、医療の検査技師などは technician と呼ばれる。

[*p.*101 *l.*7]　**screen**：「検査する」。screen A for B なら「B (病気など) を検出するために A (人・血液など) を検査する」。

174

- [*p.*101 *l.*8]　**mucus**：「(鼻や喉の) 粘液」
- [*p.*101 *l.*13]　**pouched rats**：「オニネズミ」。猫ぐらいの大きさの、尻尾の長いネズミで、ほお袋がある。pouched は「袋のある」で、pouched animal と言えばカンガルーなどの「有袋類、有袋動物」。pouch は「小袋、ポーチ」「(カンガルーなどの) 育児嚢、(リスなどの) ほお袋」。
- [*p.*101 *l.*16]　**sponsoring**：「資金提供している」。「スポンサードする」という日本語表現も出てきたが、sponsor は動詞で「資金提供する、後援する」、名詞で「スポンサー、出資者、後援者」。sponsored は形容詞で「資金提供を受けている、資金提供された」。
- [*p.*101 *l.*18]　**It makes sense.**：「なるほど、これはうなずける」。make sense は「(説明や理由などの) 理屈が通っている、意味が明瞭である、理解できる」。
- [*p.*101 *l.*18]　**sniff out**：「(警察犬などが) 匂いをかいで (薬物などを) 見つける」。sniff は「鼻をすする、匂いをかぐ、鼻から吸入する」。
- [*p.*101 *l.*20]　**olfactory**：名詞の前で「嗅覚の」。「嗅覚が鋭い」なら have a good sense of smell などと言う。
- [*p.*101 *l.*24]　**cheese will do**：「チーズで十分だろう」。That'll do.「それでも十分だ」「いいかげんにしろ」などもよく使われる表現。

Did the Dangerous Alligator Need "Anger Management"?

- [*p.*102 タイトル]　**Anger Management**：「アンガーマネジメント」。1970年代にアメリカで始まった「怒りをコントロールする心理技術」のこと。
- [*p.*102 *l.*2]　**sudden bouts of anger**：「突然の怒りの発作」「突然の発作的激怒」。bout には「(一時的な) 期間、瞬間」「(病気などの) 発作」のほかに、ボクシングやレスリングの「ひと試合」「ひと勝負」、あるいは「ひと仕事」「ひと働き」という意味もある。
- [*p.*102 *l.*5]　**therapy**：「治療」「療法」「セラピー」。shock therapy は「ショック療法」、surgical therapy は「外科療法」となる。語源はギリシャ語の *therapeía*（治療、奉仕）。
- [*p.*102 *l.*7]　**alligator**：「アリゲーター」。口語では gator とも言う。米国産のミシシッピワニなど口先が短いワニ。ナイル川やインド、オーストラリアなどに生息する口先が長いワニは crocodile、中南米に生息する比較的小さなアリゲーターは caiman「カイマン」と言う。インドのガンジス川などに生息するワニは gavial「ガビアル」と呼ばれ、ヒンズー教では神聖視されている。
- [*p.*102 *l.*14]　**rob**：「(金品を) 奪う、盗む」「強盗を働く」。暴力や恐喝など不法な方法で「奪い去る」こと。名詞は robbery「略奪、強奪」で、daylight robbery は「白昼強盗」。robber は「強盗、略奪者」、robber band は「強盗団」。類語には、steal「こっそり盗む」、sack「戦乱の中で街を破壊し金品を略奪する」、loot「無法状態の中で暴徒が略奪する」、plunder「盗賊が金品を略奪する」、shoplift「万引きする」などがある。

- [p.102 l.15] **donned**：don は「着用する、身に着ける」。「do（行う）＋ on（身に着けて）」から生まれた文語的表現。ちなみに「脱ぐ」は doff。これも「do（行う）＋ off（脱いで）」からできた動詞。
- [p.102 l.17] **case**：名詞では「箱、容器」「話題になっている事柄、ケース」「事件」などの意味があるが、ここでは動詞で「(犯行を目的として)下調べする」という口語表現。
- [p.102 l.20] **mobile**：mobile phone「携帯電話」のこと。「携帯電話」はほかに cellular phone、cellphone、あるいは cell とも言う。「彼女の携帯に電話する」は call her on her mobile phone / cellular phone / cell となる。
- [p.103 l.3] **diving into**：ここでの dive into は「～に飛び込む」「～に潜り込む」。ほかには「～に突進する」「～に没頭する」など。dive には「(飛行機や鳥が)急降下する」「(価格や価値が)急落する」という意味もある。
- [p.103 l.12] **intruders**：intruder は「(違法の)侵入者」や「(歓迎されない)邪魔者」のこと。動詞 intrude は「侵入する」「(招かれないのに)押しかける」「無理やり押し付ける」。名詞 intrusion は「(意見などの)押し付け」「侵入」「でしゃばり」などの意味。
- [p.103 l.19] **They were able to capture that angry alligator**：「彼らはその怒れるワニを捕まえることができた」。can の過去形である could ではなく were able to が使われているのは、「～できただろう」という仮定法のニュアンスが出るのを避けるため。capture は「捕まえる、捕らえる」で、類語の catch より「苦労して捕らえる」「獲得したものが誇らしく思える」というニュアンスが強い。
- [p.103 l.21] **identified**：identify は「確認する」「識別する」「突きとめる」。identify a corpse で「死体の身元を確認する」という意味になる。「鑑定する」「証明する」「同一視する」「一体感を抱く」という場合にも使用される。
- [p.103 l.22] **anatomy**：ここでは「(体の)組織」のこと。「解剖(学)」「構造」「人体」などという意味もある。生物の「組織」という意味では、ほかに tissue を使うこともある。
- [p.103 l.22] **DNA**：deoxyribonucleic acid「デオキシリボ核酸」は、染色体の中に細かく折り畳まれており、ハシゴをひねったような二重らせん構造を持つ。A（アデニン）と T（チミン）、G（グアニン）と C（シトシン）が対に結合したものを塩基対と言い、その配列が遺伝情報となる。DNA は日常的な会話においても、「先祖から子孫へ伝わるもの」、または「遺伝子」という意味で使用される。
- [p.104 l.4] **swamps**：swamp は「沼地」「湿地」。オランダ語の *zwanp*（沼地）より。動詞では「浸水させる、水浸しにする」、「(仕事や困難が)どっと押し寄せる」「忙殺される」「無力にする、途方に暮れさせる」などの意味にも。
- [p.104 l.9] **Everglades Tour**：Everglades は、フロリダ州マイアミ郊外の観光地「エバーグレーズ国立公園」のことで、世界遺産となっている。広大な湿地帯で、水深30cm程度の浅瀬が草に覆われており、River of Grass「草の川」とも呼ばれる。この tour「ツアー、旅行」

では、強力な風力エンジンを積み込んだ swamp boat / airboat「エアボート」に乗って湿地帯を疾走し、野生のアリゲーターを見ることもできる。

[p.104 *l*.13] **a patch of grass**:「草の生えた狭い土地」。patch は「1区画の土地」。「継ぎに当てる布」「(傷に当てる) 布 / 絆創膏」「眼帯」、あるいは「まだら」「(警察官の) 担当区」という意味もある。patchwork「パッチワーク」は、いろいろな布の切れ端を縫い合わせて大きな布をつくる手芸。

[p.104 *l*.16] **hauled him back by his tail**:「アリゲーターの尻尾を持って引っ張り上げた / 引きずり戻した」。haul には「運ぶ」「連れてくる」「逮捕する」「連行する」「招喚する」などという意味もある。

[p.104 *l*.18] **with apparent reluctance**:「あからさまに嫌々な様子で」。apparent は「明白な」「はっきりした」「外見上の」「見かけの」。reluctance は「気が進まないこと」「気乗り薄」「不本意」「嫌気」。with reluctance は「しぶしぶ」「嫌々ながら」、without reluctance で「喜んで」。

[p.104 *l*.19] **engaged his opponent in a strange kind of wrestling match**:「相手を奇妙なレスリングの試合に引き込んだ」。engage には「雇用する」「婚約させる」という意味があるが、ここでは「巻き込む」「携わらせる」。同時に「交戦する / させる」という意味もあり、このダブルミーニングで「アリゲーターは嫌々ながら戦わざるをえなかった」というニュアンスをユーモラスに表現している。

[p.104 *l*.21] **by holding the poor creature still with his back on the grass**:「動けないように、このあわれな動物を草むらの上に仰向けに押さえつけて」。hold は「押さえつける」、still は「静止して、動かないで」という副詞。with his back on the grass は「草の上で仰向けになって」。

[p.104 *l*.23] **a big chunk of meat**:「大きな肉の塊」。chunk は「大きい塊」「厚切り」「丸太」のこと。肉片やパン、チーズ、木材について使用されることが多い。

[p.104 *l*.25] **clapped**:clap は「(人や演技に対して) 拍手する」。もともと「ピシャリ」「バシッ」という擬音から生まれた単語。類語に applaud「拍手喝采する」がある。

[p.105 *l*.1] **trained to always swim back for another exhibition**:「もうひとつ別のショーをするために、いつも泳いで戻るよう訓練されていた」。train は「訓練する」「トレーニングする」。exhibition は「博覧会」「展覧会」のことだが、ここでは「ショー」「見世物」のこと。

[p.105 *l*.10] **take a selfie**:「自撮りをする」。selfie は「自撮り」、撮影者が手に持ったカメラで自分自身を被写体として撮影すること。take は「(写真を) 撮る」という意味。

[p.105 *l*.11] **cuddling up to**:cuddle up to ... は「〜にぴったりと寄り添う」「〜に寄り添って寝る」「〜にもたれかかる」。cuddle は「抱きしめる」「抱擁する」、名詞では「抱擁」。

[*p.*105 *l.*20] **Buddhist monastery**:「仏教の僧院」。monasteryには、「カトリックの男子修道院」という意味もある。語源はギリシャ語の*monázein*（独りで生きる）から。

[*p.*105 *l.*24] **flies off the handle**：理性のコントロールを失って「激怒する」。flyは「飛ぶ」、offは「〜から離れて」、handleは斧や鎌の「柄」「取っ手」という意味。アメリカ開拓時代に生まれた表現で、斧や鎌を振りかざして相手に殴りかかったときに勢いあまって刃が柄からスポッと抜けて相手に向かって飛んでいく様子を「精神的に制御できない怒り」にたとえた口語表現。

[*p.*106 *l.*1] **sudden outbursts**：「突然の感情の爆発／ほとばしり」。sudden angerをこのように言い換えている。outburstは「どっとあふれること」「湧き上がること」「火山の爆発」といった意味もある。

[*p.*106 *l.*6] **demanded 2 pounds ($3) for services in the ladies' comfort room**：「女性用お手洗いで、サービスのために2ポンド（3ドル）も要求された」。comfort room「心休まる場所」とは「トイレ」のことで、フィリピンで最初に言われるようになったとされる。demandは「請求する」「要求する」。海外のトイレには、おせっかいにも手を拭くタオルを渡してくれる係の人などがいて、サービス料として金銭を要求されることがある。

[*p.*106 *l.*9] **Well, you can't please everybody.**：「まあ、すべての人を満足させることはできませんよね」。ここでのpleaseは動詞で「(人を) 満足させる／喜ばせる／楽しませる」。

[*p.*107 *l.*1] **enclosure with no bare earth**：「むき出しの地面のない囲い」。ここでのenclosureは「（柵などで）囲まれた土地」。ほかには「（手紙への）同封（物）」という意味もある。動詞のencloseは「取り囲む」「囲いをする」や「（封筒や小包に）同封する」。with no bare earthは「むき出しの地面のない」。bareは「裸の、むき出しの、露出した」、earthは「地球」のことだが、ここでは「地面」「地表」のことで、コンクリートで固められた人工的な「囲い」の中で生きるゾウの悲哀を表している。

[*p.*107 *l.*6] **digestive system**：「消化器系」。digestiveは「消化の」「消化力のある」。動詞はdigest「消化する」「要約する」、名詞はdigestion「消化」「理解」だが、「要約」「ダイジェスト」という場合にはdigestとなる。systemは「(身体器官の)系統、組織」のこと。

[*p.*107 *l.*12] **signed an online petition**：「オンラインでの嘆願書に署名した」。petitionは「請願書」「嘆願」、動詞では「請願する」「請願書を出す」となる。

[*p.*108 *l.*6] **complex feelings ranging from rage and happiness to depression and loneliness**：「怒りや幸福感から憂鬱、孤独感までの多岐にわたる複雑な感情」。complexは「複雑な」。range from 〜 to ... は「〜から…に及ぶ」「〜から…まで多岐にわたる／幅がある」という意味。

It's More Fun in the Philippines ... with Lots of Money!

- [p.109 *l*.1] **bank holdups**:「銀行強盗」。holdup は名詞で「強盗」。句動詞 hold up は「拳銃などを突きつけて金品を強奪する」という意味。
- [p.109 *l*.7] **the Federal Reserve Bank of New York**:「ニューヨーク連邦準備銀行 (連銀)」。アメリカの中央銀行にあたる the Federal Reserve Board (FRB)「連邦準備理事会」が統括する連邦準備銀行のひとつ。連銀は、外国の中央銀行や政府などの口座を約 250 管理している。
- [p.109 *l*.8] **Hackers**:「ハッカー」。コンピューターやネットワークに関する高度な知識や技術を持つ人。他人のコンピューターに侵入し、データを改竄したり盗むなど、その高い技術を悪用する人の意味で使われることも多いが、セキュリティー対策など善良な目的で活動する人は特に white hacker と呼ばれる。悪いハッカーは black hacker、あるいは cracker「破壊者」などと言う。動詞は hack「ハッキングする」で、原義は「(斧などで) たたき切る、めった切りにする」「切り開く、開墾する」。
- [p.109 *l*.9] **whopping**:口語的な形容詞で「法外な、とてつもない、でかい」。a whopping big trout「ばかでかいマス」のように big や great を強調する副詞としてもよく使われる。
- [p.109 *l*.10] **foreign reserves**:「外貨準備金」。対外債務の返済や為替介入の資金として使われ、自国通貨の安定と通貨危機に備える預金や証券、金などの資産。
- [p.109 *l*.12] **robberies**:robbery は「強盗」。commit a robbery で「強盗を働く」となる。動詞は rob で「暴力や脅しを使って金品を奪う」。
- [p.109 *l*.13] **took the hit**:take the hit は口語で「被害を受ける」。この hit は名詞で「打撃」「損害」。The industry took a hit last year. で、「その業界は去年大損害を被った」となる。
- [p.109 *l*.16] **could have stolen more, much more**:「もっとはるかに多く盗むことだってできた」。「could have + 過去分詞」という仮定法過去完了の用法。過去の事実に反する仮定や想像を表す。
- [p.109 *l*.18] **feeding a demand**:feed は「(人や動物などに) 食べ物を与える」という意味だが、ここでは「コンピューターに情報を送る」。demand は「要求、請求」。つまりコンピューターに侵入してお金を請求するということ。
- [p.109 *l*.20] **as luck would have it**:「運よく、幸いにも」「運の悪いことに、不幸にも」。状況によってどちらの意味でも用いられ、はっきりさせたい場合には luck の前に good か ill を置く。
- [p.110 *l*.2] **illegal transfer**:「不正送金」。illegal は「il(非) + legal(合法な)」からなり、「不法な、非合法な」。transfer は「trans (向こうへ) + fer (運ぶ)」で、「ある場所から別の場所へ運ぶこと」。
- [p.110 *l*.5] **alert**:形容詞で「用心深い」。「油断なく注意している」というニュアンスで、名詞では「警戒」「警報」。
- [p.110 *l*.9] **it ended up having very positive consequences**:

「とても良い結果になった」。end up ...ing は「最終的に~になる」「~で終わる」。positive は「望ましい」「肯定的な」「有益な」という形容詞。consequence は「物事の成り行き、結果、影響」。形容詞の consequent は「結果として起こる、当然の」「首尾一貫した」。

[p.110 l.10] **could have drained**:「奪うこともできたかもしれない」。過去の事実に反することを想像する仮定法過去完了の用法。drain は「(雨水などを) 排水する、排出する」という意味だが、ここでは「(お金などを) 枯渇させる、食いつぶす」。名詞の drain には「排水溝」「下水管」「流出」という意味もある。ちなみに「(海外への) 頭脳流出」は韻を踏んで brain drain と言う。

[p.110 l.12] **cancellation**:名詞で「取り消し、キャンセル」。動詞は cancel「キャンセルする、取り消す」。語源はラテン語の *cancellāre*(格子状に線を引く)で、古代ローマ人が文書の一部を取り消すときに格子状の線を引いたことに由来する。

[p.110 l.14] **processed**:process は物事を「処理する、進める」、食品などを「加工する」という意味だが、ここでは「コンピューターでデータを処理する」。

[p.110 l.15] **breach the security**:「セキュリティーシステムを破る」。breach には「(城壁・防御線などを) 突破する」以外に、「(約束・規則などを) 破る、違反する」という意味もある。ちなみに bleach は「漂白する」。

[p.110 l.19] **malicious**:「悪意のある、故意の」。名詞 malice は「mal(悪い) + ice (状態)」からなり「悪意、恨み」。

[p.110 l.21] **stalking**:stalk は「そっと後をつける、忍び寄る」だが、ここでは「コンピューターの情報にこっそりアクセスする」ということ。stalker は、日本語でも「ストーカー」として定着している。

[p.111 l.2] **transmit the money**:「電信送金する」。transmit は「trans(超えて) + mit (送る)」で、「送信する、放送する」「(病気を) 伝染させる」。名詞の transmission は「伝送」「伝達」「伝言」のほか、機械類の「伝動装置、変速装置」という意味もある。

[p.111 l.4] **deposit their ill-gotten wealth**:「不正に手に入れた富を預ける」。deposit は「(銀行などにお金を) 預ける」のほかに「手付金・保証金を支払う」という意味がある。名詞では「預金、保証金、頭金」。ill-gotten は「違法・不正な手段で得た」。wealth は「富」で、類語に fortune、riches、property がある。

[p.111 l.6] **is alleged to have given the thieves her full cooperation**:「窃盗団に全面的に協力したとされる」。be alleged to ... は「~だと伝えられる」。証拠や裏付けのない事柄について使われる表現。give ... cooperation は「~に協力する」。

[p.111 l.9] **fictitious names**:「偽名」。fictitious は fiction「小説、虚構」から派生した形容詞で「架空の、ウソの」。fictitious hero は「小説の主人公」、fictitious business trip は「カラ出張」のこと。

[p.111 l.11] **came to light**:come to light は「明るみに出る」。秘密や悪事の露見、思いがけないものの発見に使われる。

[p.111 l.11] **an attempt was made to freeze the accounts**:「口

座を凍結する試みがなされた」。attempt は名詞では「試み」「挑戦」「襲撃」、動詞では「試みる」「企てる」「挑む」。freeze は「凍るほど冷たくなる」という原義から、「凍る、凍りつく」「口が重くなる」「(人が) 急に止まる」「コンピューターがフリーズする」などの意味がある。ちなみに映画「アナと雪の女王」の原題 "Frozen" は freeze の過去分詞の形容詞形用法。

[*p.111 l.17*] **she was detained**:「彼女が拘束された」。detain は「(容疑者などを) 拘留する」「引き留める」。イギリス英語では「(病院に) 収容する」という意味もある。名詞 detention は「拘留、拘置」「(生徒の) 放課後の居残り」。detention center は「(難民などの) 収容センター」「拘置所」。

[*p.111 l.19*] **subordinates testified**:「部下たちが証言した」。subordinate は「部下」「服従者」。形容詞では「下位の、服従している」を意味する。この testify は「証言する」。ほかに「証明する」という意味もある。

[*p.111 l.21*] **take-away**:「お持ち帰りの食べ物」。アメリカでは take-out、takeout を使うことが多い。句動詞の take away は「持ち去る、連れ去る、旅行に連れ出す」だが、「(食べ物を) 買って持ち帰る」という意味もある。

[*p.111 l.25*] **called upon to ...**:call upon to ... は「〜することを正式に求める」。call on to とも言う。この文では called の前に she was が略されている。

[*p.112 l.2*] **because of self-incrimination**:「みずからを有罪にすることになるかもしれないので」。self-incrimination は法律用語で「自己負罪」、つまり自分の証言がみずからを罪に陥れること。

[*p.112 l.5*] **red flag**:「危険信号」「危険を知らせるシグナル」。共産主義・社会主義を象徴する「革命旗」「赤旗」という意味もある。

[*p.112 l.8*] **higher-ups**:ここでは「上役、上司、ボス」のこと。「首脳、高官」という意味もある。

[*p.112 l.11*] **disappear into thin air**:「跡形もなく消える」「雲散霧消する」。「空気に混じって薄くなるようにどこかに消えてしまう」というニュアンス。ちなみに「どこからともなく現れる」は appear out of thin air。

[*p.112 l.18*] **palatial**:名詞の palace「宮殿」から派生した形容詞で「宮殿のような、壮麗な」。

[*p.112 l.18*] **money laundering**:「資金洗浄、マネーロンダリング」。不正に入手したお金をさまざまに経由させて出所をわからなくすること。動詞 launder は「洗濯する」。laundry は「クリーニング店」「洗濯物」。

[*p.112 l.20*] **are exempt from ...**:「〜を免除されている」。exempt は形容詞で「免除された」、動詞では「免除する」。名詞 exemption は「免除、控除」で、tax exemption は「免税」という意味。

[*p.113 l.4*] **what there is of it**:言い換えれば、there is not much of it で「私にお金があるとしても、たいしてないので関係ないが」という軽口。

[p.113 l.7] **converted**：convert は「変える」だが、ここでは「換金する」。「改宗させる、(主義を) 転向させる」という意味もある。ほかには、野球で「選手のポジションを変える」、ラグビーでは「トライのあとキックによって得点を追加する」など。

[p.113 l.13] **Monopoly**：「モノポリー」。普通名詞の monopoly は「独占、専売」という意味。ここではすごろくのようなボードゲームのことで、不動産売買などの経済活動を行い、富を独占した人が勝ち、ほかの人は破産する。

[p.113 l.14] **identity of the Mr. Big**：「例の黒幕の正体」。identity は「アイデンティティー」「自己同一性」などという日本語にもなっているが、ここでは「身元、素性」のこと。この the は「あの〜」「くだんの〜」というふうに、話題になっている人を指し示す定冠詞。Mr. Big は「大物、実力者、黒幕」。

[p.113 l.15] **orchestrated**：ここの orchestrate は「画策する」。「オーケストラ用に編曲・作曲する」から転じて「(複雑な計画などを) 組織する、整理する、(周到に) 準備する、精緻に組み上げる」という意味になった。

[p.113 l.21] **millionaire**：「億万長者」。19 世紀中頃にフランス語から英語になった言葉と言われる。アメリカの新聞記者がある大富豪の死亡記事の執筆中に、その富の莫大さを表す表現を考えあぐねていたが、締め切りに間に合いそうになかったため、フランス語の *millionnaire*（百万長者）を借用した。英語になって一般化する過程で、n がひとつ脱落して millionaire というつづりが定着したとされる。

[p.113 l.21] **high roller**：「ギャンブルで向こう見ずな勝負をしかけて大金を賭ける人」、「金遣いの荒い人」。roll は動詞で「(さいころを) 転がす」。

[p.114 l.3] **engaged in "monkey business"**：「"いかさま商売"をしている」。engaged の前に who are が省略されている。be engaged in は「〜に従事している」。monkey business は「インチキ、いかさま、詐欺」。ポール・オースターなどを手がける翻訳家・柴田元幸氏がかつて責任編集をしていた文芸誌のタイトルが『モンキービジネス』だった。

[p.114 l.4] **account for ...**：ここでは「〜について説明する、明らかにする」。

[p.114 l.6] **take shelter**：「一時避難する」。shelter は「避難場所、(風雨や日差しを) しのぐ場所」。nuclear shelter は「核シェルター」。

[p.114 l.7] **compliant**：「従順な」という形容詞。「自己主張がなく人の言いなりになる」という意味合いが強い。名詞の compliance は「法令順守、コンプライアンス」として日本語にもなっている。

[p.114 l.7] **Gloria Macapagal Arroyo**：グロリア・マカパガル・アロヨ元フィリピン大統領 (任期 2001 – 2010)。2011 年持病の治療のために出国しようとしていたところ認められず、選挙妨害の容疑で逮捕された。翌 12 年、入院中に公金不正流用の疑いで再逮捕されたが、ドゥテルテ政権下の 18 年、下院議長に就任。

[p.114 l.10] **apprehended**：この apprehend は「逮捕する」。

arrest より形式ばった法律用語。ほかには「理解する」「心配する」「恐れる」といった意味もある。

[p.114 l.17] **exorbitant**：「法外な、途方もない」。exorbitant luxury で「途方もない贅沢」。名詞の exorbitance は「(数や程度が)過度なこと、法外なこと」。

[p.114 l.20] **gambling dens**：「賭博部屋」。den は「(キツネなどの)ねぐら」だが、「小部屋」「書斎」「隠れ家」といった意味もある。

[p.114 l.23] **ambience**：「(高級な)雰囲気」。「周辺の様子」という意味もあり、形容詞の ambient は「周囲の、環境の」。

[p.115 l.5] **one local gambler I spoke to said**：I spoke to が前の one local gambler にかかっている。つまり「私が話しかけた地元のギャンブラーのひとり」が主語で、それに said「言った」という動詞が続いている。

[p.116 l.2] **fruit machines**：slot machine「スロットマシン」のこと。バナナやサクランボ、パイナップル、ブドウなど同じ果物の絵が一列に並ぶとたくさんのコインを獲得できるため、このように表現している。

[p.116 l.6] **One media account has ...**：「あるメディアは〜としている」。account は「説明」「物語」だが、ここでは「報道」「記事」のこと。newspaper account で「新聞記事」。この has は「〜としている」「〜と語っている」という意味。

[p.116 l.16] **small cogs in a giant machinery**：「大きな機械の中の小さな歯車」という意味で、ここでは「大組織の中で小さな役割しか担っていないちっぽけな個人」といった意味。cog は「歯車」のこと。

[p.116 l.24] **how it all pans out**：「すべては、どういう結果になるのか」。pan は平べったい「鍋」のことで、句動詞 pan out は砂や砂利をその鍋で洗って砂金と分離し「砂金を産出する」から「結果が出る」という意味になった。pan out well は「うまくいく」。

Are Cows Causing Climate Change?

[p.117 タイトル] **Climate Change**：「気候変化、気候変動」。専門的にはいくつかの定義・訳語があるようだが、広くは global warming「地球温暖化」とそれによる極端な天候などの影響を指す。

[p.117 l.4] **pollution**：「汚染、公害」「汚染物質」。air pollution なら「大気汚染」、water pollution なら「水質汚染」、chemical pollution なら「化学汚染」。contamination も「汚染」だが、細菌や毒物などによる汚染に使われる。

[p.117 l.7] **is hardly ever considered**：「到底思いもよらないものだ」。hardly ever ... は「めったに〜ない、ほとんど〜ない」。consider は「〜だと考える、〜を考慮に入れる」。

[p.117 l.10] **methane-filled farts**：「メタンガスいっぱいのおなら」。methane は「メタン」。-filled は「〜でいっぱいの」。fart は「おなら」「おならをする」。ちなみに「おなら」は「屁」の婉曲表現「お鳴らし」

からきており、音がするものがおなら、音のしないものが屁だという。英語にも fart「屁」を使った I don't give a fart about it.「そんなことは屁とも思わない」という表現があるのが面白い。

- [p.117 *l*.13] **greenhouse gases**：二酸化炭素、メタン、フロンなどの「温室効果ガス、温暖化ガス」。greenhouse は「温室」。
- [p.117 *l*.14] **emitted**：「排出される」。emit は「(ガスなどを)排出する、(音や光などを)発する」。
- [p.117 *l*.17] **carbon dioxide**：「二酸化炭素」。carbon は「炭素」だが、これだけで二酸化炭素を表すことがあり、carbon emissions といえば「二酸化炭素排出量」。
- [p.118 *l*.1] **best of all**：「いちばんいいのは、何よりいいのは」。副詞的に文に挿入される表現。
- [p.118 *l*.3] **atmosphere**：「雰囲気」としておなじみの語だが、ここでは「大気」、ほかに「大気圏」も指す。
- [p.118 *l*.5] **population**：「個体数」。人なら「人口」。
- [p.118 *l*.8] **collective**：「総〜、(個々を合わせた)全体の」。動詞形は collect「集める」「集合させる」。
- [p.118 *l*.9] **in the short term**：「短期的には」。term は「期間」。long term は「長期」、medium term は「中期」。
- [p.118 *l*.15] **burping**：「げっぷ」。burp は「げっぷ(をする)」。
- [p.118 *l*.19] **mouth-watering steaks**：「よだれが出そうなステーキ」。mouth-watering は「よだれが出そうな、おいしそうな」。steak は「ステーキ」。
- [p.118 *l*.20] **cattle ranchers**：「牛の畜産農家」。cattle は集合的に「(家畜の)牛」を指す言葉で、複数形にしない。rancher は「牧場主、牧場労働者」。
- [p.119 *l*.1] **marbled**：「大理石模様の、霜降りの」。marble は「大理石」。
- [p.119 *l*.2] **reign supreme**：「最も優勢である、最高位を占める」。reign は「君臨する、行き渡る」。supreme は「最高の」。
- [p.119 *l*.5] **spoil my appetite**：「私の食欲がなくなる」。spoil は「甘やかす」でおなじみだが、「(物事を)だめにする、損なう」こと。appetite は「食欲」。spoil one's appetite は「食欲をなくさせる」。
- [p.119 *l*.8] **emanating**：「発生する」。emanate は「(音・気体・光などが)生じる、出る」。
- [p.119 *l*.9] **is being carried out**：「実施されている」。carry out は「(調査などを)実施する、行う」。
- [p.119 *l*.12] **eliminate**：「(不必要な物や人を)排除する」
- [p.119 *l*.14] **digest seaweed**：「海藻を消化する」。digest は「(食物を)消化する」。seaweed は「海草、海藻」。
- [p.119 *l*.18] **putting large airtight plastic bubbles over cows**：「大きな密閉したビニール風船を牛の背にくくり付けること」。ここでのover ... は「(覆うように〜の)上に」で、〜の上に接している状態。airtight は「密閉した、気密の」。「相手に隙を見せない、完璧な」という意味もあり、airtight alibi といえば「完璧なアリバイ」。plasticは「プラスチック(製の)、ビニール(製の)」で、plastic bag なら「ポ

リ袋、レジ袋」。bubble は「泡」を思い浮かべるが、「球状・ドーム状のもの、(患者用の)ビニールテント、(プールなどの)ドーム型構造物」なども指す。

- [p.119 l.19] **trap**：trap といえば「わな、策略」だが、ここでは動詞で「(気体や液体を)閉じ込める」。
- [p.119 l.21] **generating electricity**：「発電」
- [p.120 l.7] **wares**：ware は通常複数形で「商品、製品、陶器」のことで、ここでは「(路上や市場での)売り物」。
- [p.120 l.8] **munches away**：munch away は「むしゃむしゃ食べる」。この away には「(休まず)ずっと」「完全になくなるまで」といった意味がある。ちなみに大文字から始まる Munch は「叫び」でおなじみの画家ムンク。
- [p.120 l.14] **polite society**：「上流社会」。polite は「丁寧な、上品な」「上流の、教養のある」。society は「社会、階層、〜界」。
- [p.121 l.1] **vulgar**：「下品な、卑猥な、無作法な」
- [p.121 l.2] **pass wind**：pass / break wind は「おならをする、放屁する、(体内の)ガスが出る」。
- [p.121 l.6] **euphemism**：「婉曲表現」
- [p.121 l.7] **disguise**：「(外見や性質を)変える、隠す、ごまかす」
- [p.121 l.9] **domestic helpers**：「家政婦、家政夫」
- [p.121 l.10] **employ**：「(手法や技術を)使う、利用する」
- [p.121 l.14] **I'm afraid we'll have to let you go.**：「あなたにはお辞めいただかないと」。let you go は本来「出て行きたがっているあなたを行かせる」こと。
- [p.121 l.15] **white lie**：人を傷つけないようについた「悪意のないウソ」。これに対して black lie は、人を陥れるような「悪意のあるウソ」。
- [p.121 l.23] **ethnic cleansing**：「民族浄化」
- [p.122 l.6] **are being persecuted**：「迫害されている」。persecute は「(宗教や理念の違いで)迫害する」。
- [p.122 l.14] **call a spade a spade**：「ありのままに言う、あからさまに言う」。文字どおりには「鋤を鋤と呼ぶ」。

Improve Your English with Shakespeare!

- [p.123 l.3] **marked**：動詞 mark の中心的な意味は「痕跡をつける」「印をつける」だが、ここでは「記念する」「祝う」という意味。カレンダーに印をつけて記念日であることを示すイメージ。
- [p.123 l.3] **Scholars**：「学者」。ラテン語の *schola*「学校」+ *-ar*「の人」という成り立ちの語。「奨学生」の意味もあり、Fulbright scholar なら「フルブライト奨学生」。「奨学金」は scholarship。
- [p.123 l.5] **drinking session**：「飲み会」。session の語源は「座っていること」(sitting)で、「会合」「集会」などの意味がある。be (now) in session で「(議会が)開会中だ、(裁判が)開廷している」。ちなみに、壮絶なジャズ音楽家魂を描いた、アカデミー賞3部門受賞の映画「セッション」の原題は Session ではなく、"Whiplash"「(ド

ラマー特有の) むちうち症、鞭撻」。

[p.124 l.5] **contribution**：contribution と言えば「貢献」という印象が強いが、ここでは「(新聞・雑誌への) 投稿記事、寄稿」という意味。もともとこのエッセイは月刊誌のために書かれたので、このような表現になっている。

[p.124 l.14] **the Bard**：bard は「(古代の) 楽人」「詩人」。大文字で the Bard とするとシェークスピアを指す。

[p.124 l.14] **coined**：名詞の coin は「硬貨」だが、動詞では「(新しい語や表現を) 創り出す」「(硬貨を) 鋳造する」。

[p.124 l.16] **Brexit**：「Britain + exit」からなる、「英国の EU 離脱」を表す造語 (coined word)。国民投票後に離脱を悔いる Bregret (Britain + regret) という語も現れた。

[p.124 l.17] **TO BE, OR NOT TO BE**："Hamlet"「ハムレット」で、ハムレットは父を殺した男が義父と知り、生きるか、そんな世に別れを告げるか、To be, or not to be – that is the question.「生きるべきか死ぬべきかーそれが問題だ」と苦悩する。

[p.124 l.21] **slaves**：slave「奴隷」の語源は Slav「スラブ人」。中世にスラブ人が奴隷にされたことから。英国の夏のクラシック音楽祭 The Proms などで、会場全体で大合唱される愛国的な歌 Rule, Britannia「統べよ、ブリタニア」のリフレインに、Rule, Britannia! Britannia, rule the waves: Britons never, never, never shall be slaves.「統べよ、ブリタニア、ブリタニアよ、大海原を支配せよ。ブリトン人は決して奴隷にはなるまじ」とある。Britannia は英国を擬人化した女神「ブリタニア」、Britons は「古代のブリトン人」「英国人」。

[p.124 l.23] **EAT US OUT OF HOUSE AND HOME**："Henry IV Part II"「ヘンリー四世 第2部」の He hath eaten me out of house and home. から。太っちょ騎士フォルスタッフに金をだまし取られ、食いつぶされた、と居酒屋の女将がこぼす。eat A out of house and home「A (の財産) を食いつぶす」という成句になっている。

[p.125 l.4] **A DISH FIT FOR THE GODS**："Julius Caesar"「ジュリアス・シーザー」の Let's carve him as a dish fit for the gods. から。シーザー暗殺の密談中にブルータスが、たたき切るのではなく神々にささげるにふさわしい死にざまにするのだ、と語る。carve は「切り分ける」、a dish fit for the gods は「最高の供え物」。

[p.125 l.12] **BETTER TO BE THREE HOURS TOO SOON THAN ONE MINUTE TOO LATE**："The Merry Wives of Windsor"「ウィンザーの陽気な女房たち」の better three hours too soon than a minute too late「1分遅れるより 3 時間早いほうがいい」から。

[p.125 l.16] **COME WHAT MAY**："Macbeth"「マクベス」の Come what come may,/Time and the hour runs through the roughest day. から。魔女たちの言葉どおり、自分がコーダ領主になると知ったマクベスが「来るものは来るがいい。荒れ狂う嵐の日にも時は流れていくのだ」と独白する。一般に come what may の形で使われ、「何があろうと」という意味。

- [*p.*125 *l.*20] **prenuptial agreement**：「婚前契約」。結婚する前にあらかじめ、離婚した場合の財産分与などさまざまなことを取り決めておくもの。antenuptial contract とも言う。prenuptial は「婚前の、婚姻前の」で、pre-「前の」＋ nuptial「結婚の」。nuptial は硬い言葉で「結婚（式）の」「婚礼、華燭の典」という意味の形容詞・名詞。agreement は「契約、協定、同意」。

- [*p.*125 *l.*23] **A FOOL'S PARADISE**："Romeo and Juliet"「ロミオとジュリエット」の if ye should lead her into a fool's paradise から。ジュリエットの乳母（Nurse）がロミオに「愚者の楽園にジュリエットを連れていくなんて」とんでもないよ、とたしなめる。live / be in a fool's paradise は「先のことも考えず、一時の幸せに浸る」こと。

- [*p.*126 *l.*9] **IT'S HIGH TIME**："The Comedy of Errors"「間違いの喜劇」にある'tis high time that I were hence「引き揚げる潮時だ」から。it's high time ... は言い換えると it's about time ... で、「〜してもいいころだ」「〜するなら今でしょ」という表現。

- [*p.*127 *l.*1] **I'm IN A PICKLE**："The Tempest"「嵐」のナポリ王アロンゾと道化トリンキュローとのやり取り "How camest thou in this pickle?" "I have been in such a pickle since ..."「何故かような目に遭っておるのだ」「こんなやっかいなことになりましたのは……」から。pickle は漬け物の「ピクルス」のこと。野菜やスパイスが混ざった混沌状態から be in a pickle は「面倒な状況にある、窮地に陥る」という意味になったと言われる。be in a mess と同義。

- [*p.*127 *l.*6] **BROKE THE ICE by cracking a joke**："The Taming of the Shrew"「じゃじゃ馬ならし」に出てくる And if you break the ice ... より。break the ice は氷を割るのではなく「場を和ませる」という意味。icebreaker は「初対面の緊張をほぐす軽い話題や冗談」。crack は「ひびが入る」「ポンと割る」が元の意味で、crack a joke で「冗談を飛ばす」。

- [*p.*127 *l.*24] **DIDN'T SLEEP A WINK**：喜劇 "Cymbeline"「シンベリン」の Since I received command to do this business I have not slept one wink.「このご用を言いつかりましてから、一睡もできませんでした」から。a wink はここでは片目でするウィンクではなく、「目を閉じること、ひと眠り」。「ひと眠りする、昼寝する」は take a nap だが、take a wink とも言う。

- [*p.*128 *l.*4] **ALL THAT GLITTERS IS NOT GOLD**："The Merchant of Venice"「ヴェニスの商人」から。ポーシャの求婚者のひとりで金・銀・銅の箱の中から金の箱を選んだモロッコ公。箱を開けて出てきたのが All that glitters is not gold.「光る物必ずしも金ならず」と書かれた巻物だった。今にもこの言葉はことわざとして通用している。glitter は「光が反射してきらきら光る」こと。

- [*p.*128 *l.*9] **GREEK TO ME**："Julius Caesar" で、「キケロは何か言っていたか」と問うキャシアスに、現場にいたキャスカが for mine own part, it was Greek to me.「わたしにとってはちんぷんかんぷんでした」と答えたところから。秘密が漏れないようにキケロは外

国語であるギリシャ語で話していたので、キャスカには理解できなかった。It's Greek to me. は「さっぱりわからない」と言いたいときに使えるちょっとしゃれた便利な表現。

[p.128 l.17] **HAD SEEN BETTER DAYS**："As You Like It"「お気に召すまま」で、身内に追放され零落した公爵が「たしかにかつては確たる身分もあったが」と振り返る True is it that we have seen better days ... から。have seen better days は「(人や物が)かつてはいい時代があった」という表現。

[p.128 l.23] **LOVE IS BLIND**：シェークスピア作品にたびたび登場することわざだが、有名なのは "Romeo and Juliet" のマーキュシオの If love be blind, love cannot hit the mark.「もし恋が盲目なら、恋は的を射ることができない」というセリフ。ただ、この love は「恋」ではなくローマ神話の恋の神「キューピッド」とも解釈できる。"A Midsummer Night's Dream"「真夏の夜の夢」には、Love looks not with the eyes, but with the mind; And therefore is wing'd Cupid painted blind.「恋は目でするのではなく、心でするもの。だから羽のあるキューピッドは目が見えない姿で描かれているの」というセリフがある。目をつぶっていたり目隠しをしたりして矢を放とうとするキューピッドがしばしば絵画に登場する。

[p.129 l.4] **ALL'S WELL THAT ENDS WELL**：「終わりよければすべてよし」。シェークスピアの喜劇作品の題名になっている。All is well that ends well を分解すると、that ends well が関係代名詞節、主語 All が先行詞で、「うまく終わるものすべてがよい」。

[p.129 l.9] **VANISHED INTO THIN AIR**：vanish into thin air は「跡形もなく消える」。"Othello"「オセロ」では、道化が go; vanish into air; away!「さあ行った行った、消えろ！」と楽師たちを追い払う。"The Tempest" では、プロスペローのセリフに spirits ... are melted into air, into thin air「妖精たちは空に紛れてしまった、跡形もなくな」とある。この thin は「(気体が)薄い、希薄な」。

[p.129 l.12] **TO MY HEART'S CONTENT**：to one's heart's content は「〜の心ゆくまで」。content は「満足」。シェークスピアの詩 "Venus and Adonis"「ヴィーナスとアドニス」の献辞に I leave it to your honourable survey, and your honour to your heart's content.「伯爵様のご吟味に託します。お心ゆきますままに」とある。

[p.129 l.18] **LAUGHINGSTOCK**：「物笑い」。"The Merry Wives of Windsor" に Pray you, let us not be laughing-stocks to other men's humours.「頼むから、わしらがほかの連中の笑いの種にならんようにしてくれよ」というセリフがある。

[p.129 l.24] **A GOOD RIDDANCE**：悲劇 "Troilus and Cressida"「トロイラスとクレシダ」にあるセリフで、「(特定の人がいなくなって)せいせいした」「いいやっかい払いだ」。riddance「除去、やっかい払い」は、現在ではほぼこのフレーズでしか使われない。

Brian Powle's
Unbelievable World
―――――――――――――――――――――――

2019年11月15日　第1刷発行

著　者　Brian W. Powle
　　　　Ⓒ 2019 Brian W. Powle
発行者　森永公紀
発行所　NHK出版
　　　　〒150-8081 東京都渋谷区宇田川町41-1
　　　　電話：0570-002-046（編集）
　　　　　　　0570-000-321（注文）
　　　　ホームページ　http://www.nhk-book.co.jp
　　　　振替 00110-1-49701

印　刷　研究社印刷 / 近代美術

製　本　二葉製本

定価はカバーに表示してあります。
落丁・乱丁本はお取り替えいたします。

本書の無断複写（コピー）は、著作権法上の例外を除き、著作権侵害となります。
Printed in Japan
ISBN 978-4-14-035164-2　C0082

ユーモアたっぷりに日本とイギリスを比較

"Secrets" of England

NHK語学テキスト「遠山顕の英会話楽習」で連載中の著者の英文エッセイ集がついに刊行。NHK出版新書『マインド・ザ・ギャップ！』の英語版に、EU離脱問題のエッセイをプラス。日本を知り尽くした著者による、ユニークな「英国の秘密」を英文でお楽しみください。

発売中

"Secrets" of England

コリン・ジョイス著
●定価 本体 **1,100**円+税

[主な内容]

- The Treasures of British Cuisine （イギリス料理の宝）
- The Sniffer's Guide to Japan （日本の「匂い」案内）
- Miscellaneous Strange Habits of the English （イギリス人の奇妙な癖）
- The Japan I Didn't Like （ぼくが好きになれなかったニッポン）
- "The Wetherspoons Brexit Test" （「チェーン居酒屋」でブレクジットテスト）
など26章

NHK出版

世界のあちこちで起こったオドロキの出来事!
ロングセラー "My Humorous" シリーズの
著者が贈る辞書ナシで読める英語エッセイ。

Brian Powle's
Amazing World News
Text & Cartoons Brian W. Powle

- 定価 本体 **1,000** 円+税
- 新書判 並製・160ページ

日本では報道されない驚愕のニュースを
ウィットとペーソスを交えて描く
『NHKニュースで英会話』で評判の連載、待望の出版化。

電子書籍版も発売

Brian Powleの既刊本

発売中

- My Humorous Japan
- My Humorous Japan Part 2
- My Humorous Japan Part 3

NHK出版